THE FOUR YOGAS OF ENLIGHTENMENT©

GUIDE TO DON JUAN'S NAGUALISM & ESOTERIC BUDDHISM

EDWARD PLOTKIN

The Four Yogas Of Enlightenment:
Guide To Don Juan's Nagualism & Esoteric Buddhism
ISBN: 0972087907

Edward Plotkin
FourYogas.com
318 Main Street
Madison, NJ 07940-2355
Email: info@FourYogas.com.

CONTENTS

1. THE MASTERY OF AWARENESS

Stopping the World

On a day forever etched in my memory I unexpectedly discovered the extraordinary teachings of the Yaqui Indian seer, don Juan. While looking for something new and interesting to read, I had unknowingly stumbled upon a treasure trove of mystic lore and esoteric knowledge. After a few weeks of studying don Juan's teachings I became mesmerized by the wise old Indian's words. I slowly began to discover that don Juan was a magnificent *warrior* and *man of knowledge.* His mysterious teachings revealed a path to the mastery of awareness. I had been completely unaware that man had access to higher states of consciousness or that a path through the mastery of awareness to enlightened being existed. Having had little or no interest in the subject of altered states of awareness, it seemed unlikely that my personal world and interests were about to profoundly change. During the next few years as I studied don Juan's teachings, as brilliantly expounded in the writings of his disciple Carlos Castaneda, a number of exceptional experiences in non-ordinary reality occurred.

The first of these events involved a radical shift and permanent change in my perception of the nature of time. The significance of this had far reaching effects, and was an incredible impetus for the metamorphosis in consciousness that was about to occur. For if time was not the regular linear expansion that I had always taken for granted, then belief in the absolute nature of my perceived world and personal self was in jeopardy.

My experience can best be described as an implosion of awareness wherein the world had stopped. As my awareness came to an absolute standstill I noticed that as long as my focus did not move off absolute center that time had no duration, memory was barely a sliver, and that the universe was arising solely and uniquely as a function of my perception. A tiny shift in the assemblage point of awareness brought with it an expansion of both a perceived historical world and personal self, as well as a heightened realization that the unfolding of these worlds were synchronous with movements away from the absolute center of awareness. The world and self could be seen to be arising as modifications in consciousness. Once this witness-position is attained in meditative absorption, or heightened awareness, these movements of the assemblage point of awareness are seen to be non-binding modifications in consciousness, and without duration or lasting relationship to the "I" at the center of perception. A seer, or don Juan, would see this as being the time of the double.

> "Once it has learned to dream the double, the self arrives at this weird crossroad and a moment comes when he realizes that it is the double who dreams the self." [1]
> Tales Of Power, Carlos Castaneda

Later, I learned that this event was a glimpse at the first of the four yogas, the one-pointed yoga or cosmic consciousness. This was followed during subsequent years by a series of alterations and expansions running through the range of all of my senses, and a journey in consciousness through each of the four yogas and the psychological formation and integration of the self. My internship in the meditative exploration of time, self, and the very nature of reality itself had begun in earnest.

The various teachings presented in this book have been accessed and assimilated while in meditative absorption, or in don Juan's terminology heightened awareness. Learning to stop the world, bringing cohesiveness to movements of the assemblage point through discerning wisdom, and specifically the transformation from egoic-self to enlightened Being through the mastery of nondual awareness are the dominant themes of The Four Yogas Of Enlightenment.

> "What happens to the persons whose assemblage points loses rigidity?" I asked. "If they're not warriors, they think they're losing their minds." [2]
> The Fire From Within, Carlos Castaneda

Meditating on the teachings of different masters and traditions can synergistically enhance *heightened awareness*. With understanding achieved in more than one tradition, cross verification of terms and states of consciousness can be correlated. Without correlation, progress is exceedingly difficult because there is no contrasting point of view with which one can glean the intended meaning, nor a deeper understanding. The Four Yogas Of Enlightenment guides the reader along the meditative path to enlightenment through transcendence of the ego, spiritual awakening, and the stabilization and mastery of transcendental awareness. This book explores enlightenment, the spiritual path to radical sanity and infinite love, in an informal but informed and accessible manner.

While every effort has been made to make The Four Yogas both introductory and progressive, these teachings can be best accessed by average to advanced students of consciousness exploration and expansion. Adi Da, a supremely enlightened Western born avatar, discusses the issue of exercising the discriminative mind in order to realize the transcendental position of awareness in the introduction to Self-Realization Of Noble Wisdom: The Lankavatara Sutra:

> It is a kind of "Catch 22" literature. You know that the Truth is ultimate transcendence of the discriminative mind, but in order to realize the transcendence of the discriminative mind, you must already have realized the transcendence of the discriminative mind! [3]

Nevertheless, let us assume that we have experienced sufficient transcendence and continue our quest. The undertaking of the transcendence of egoic mind is an awesome but not impossible task. The beginning of enlightenment and the end of self-inflicted neurotic thinking is within the grasp of anyone willing to learn how to still the discursive mind and then study the resultant state with full awareness. In fact, it is not until one has gained sufficient meditative distance from the verbal dimensions of consciousness through meditative silence that one can begin to gauge the neurotic dimensions of egoic mind.

The ideal state to study consciousness is found at the juncture of meditative absorption and discerning awareness, the equivalent to don Juan's heightened awareness. The journey towards the mastery of awareness begins by stilling the mind, while single-pointedly stabilizing the assemblage point in heightened awareness, thereby stopping the world. At this position in awareness consciousness studies consciousness itself, revealing the hidden and ultimate nature of time, self, and reality. The apprentice sorcerer while in heightened awareness and having stopped the world clearly sees the inner luminous path to becoming a seer and man or woman of knowledge.

> *Inner silence works from the moment you begin to accrue it. The desired result is what the old sorcerers called stopping the world, the moment when everything around us ceases to be what it's been.*
> *It is this moment when man the slave becomes man the free being, capable of feats of perception that defy our linear imagination.*[4]
> *The Active Side Of Infinity, Carlos Castaneda*

Reconstructing Enlightenment

The Four Yogas Of Enlightenment presents a reconstruction of the stages of awareness leading to enlightenment and leads the reader progressively away from neurotic self-construction through the union of meditative absorption and discerning awareness. The union of meditative absorption and discerning awareness is a special state of heightened awareness that is explored and clarified in the pages of this book, and can be viewed as an achievement in consciousness arrived at and stabilized through continued practice in meditative absorption and simultaneous study of the teachings of master seers.

Although the terminology of various masters may be difficult to access at first, with continued practice clarity is enhanced, and discerning awareness flowers. Many of the passages mentioned herein at first seemed to me to be impenetrable. However, when assimilated over time, magnificent teachings and wondrous states of awareness arced across the sky of mind, and my progress was immeasurably enhanced.

Perhaps those who do not meditate, or have never experienced altered states of reality, may find it difficult to believe that extraordinary states of awareness and the seed of transformative growth are available within consciousness. However not believing, or never having had the experience does not alter the hidden truth. For example, if you do not speak French you would have to study for some time before you could assimilate unfamiliar sounds. However, prior to your understanding, it would not be accurate to deny the existence of meaning within the French language simply because it was not within your current understanding. There are newfound states of consciousness to be grasped, practiced and finally mastered in meditative absorption, and their existence can only be discovered and mastered through our own effort.

> *"I've said that the new seers believed that the assemblage point can be moved from within. They went one step further and maintained that impeccable men need no one to guide them, that by themselves, through saving their energy, they can do everything seers do."* [5]
> *The Fire From Within,* Carlos Castaneda

Transcending the Dust of Time and Knowledge

One of the major difficulties the student of *heightened awareness* has is to bring a degree of cohesiveness to the newly found factors in consciousness. For the skilled meditator the requisite cohesiveness can be provided by means of consciousness studying consciousness from the perspective of a variety of meditation languages. The next stage is completed when the tonal and the nagual, or the egoic and transcendental aspects of awareness are brought into balance and harmony. Unbending intent coupled with an open and flexible approach to acquiring and assimilating seemingly disparate teachings are key factors in maintaining progress along the inner path to transcendental wisdom.

It is in the final stages of yogic awareness that the egoic mind continues to function and serve the needs of the self in the world, however the egoic mind is no longer in absolute control. The emergent man or woman of knowledge establishes a new way of being as the giver of knowledge, not the keeper; the source of love, not the seeker. The inconceivable transformation-death of old mind, with its endless labyrinth-like soliloquies and false projections, is replaced by transcendental mind. The seed from within has flowered and the path to Self mastery is in view. The guru within, obscured until now by egoic mind, can proceed along the stages of yogic awareness and development.

My recognition of the necessity of a book organizing and clarifying these teachings came about as I wrestled with understanding yogic knowledge and altered states of awareness. However, it soon became apparent that not only is progress slow and difficult to achieve, it is perhaps even more difficult to speak or write about states of consciousness that are beyond the ordinary realms of language. I realized that I required either a personal guru or a means of enhancing my understanding through expanded effort. A relationship with a guru never materialized and other and perhaps more powerful means of continuing my education appeared. In retrospect it seems that when each stage of my development in consciousness exploration stabilized a new and more powerful teaching became available.

During the mid-eighties the exiled Tibetans began to disseminate the written teachings of the great sages of Tibetan Buddhism. The translation of these extraordinary teachings into English was another serendipitous occurrence for me. Just as I had reached some major impasses in my studies of don Juan's lessons many marvelous Tibetan Buddhist teachings texts became available. Of particular interest were texts illuminating both the gradual and instantaneous path instructions of realized sages. These teachings revealed a cohesive knowledge and systematic path leading to the attainment of a radically quiescent mind, and instructive guidance for seeing and analyzing the true and apparent nature of consciousness and reality. I could see striking parallels with the teachings of don Juan, and realized that I had once again found lessons in the way of the warrior embodying Self-realized qualities such as fearlessness, serenity, wisdom, and compassion.

> *Contemplate the three planes of existence [past, present, and future] as being of mental origin, since they are designated by the mind. By analyzing the mind, the meditator examines the essence of things.* [6]
> *The first Bhavanakrama*

> *"Was it something I will see in the future?" I asked. "There's no future!" he exclaimed cuttingly.*
> *"The future is only a way of talking. For a sorcerer there is only the here and now."* [7]
> *Tales Of Power, Carlos Castaneda*

The Mastery of Transcendental Awareness

The Four Yogas Of Enlightenment illuminates the sublimely transcendental stages of awareness of Tibetan Buddhism. In contrast with Buddhism, I examine the way of the warrior, and the mastery of luminous awareness as elaborated in the writings of Carlos Castaneda. I have also drawn upon and revealed the mystic teachings of the Kashmir Shaivism school of nondual awareness. In my final chapters I correlate the most advanced, esoteric, and incomparable states of samadhic awareness of the Western avatar and living Buddhist master, Adi Da, with the quintessence of don Juan's Nagualism and Chinese and Tibetan Buddhism.

> *Until The Ajna Door Is Fully Opened (or Otherwise Fully Transcended By Native Identification With The Witness-Position Of Consciousness), It Is Truly, the Ajna Knot.*[8]
> *The Dawn Horse Testament, Adi Da*

> *The Discipline In the First Stage Of the Perfect Practice Is To Stand As The Witness-Consciousness.*
> *The Discipline In the Second Stage Of the Perfect Practice Is Deep Contemplation Of Consciousness and Deep Identification With Consciousness Itself.* [9]
> *The Dawn Horse Testament, Adi Da*

That which we in the West consider to be completed adult development, is considered by both Eastern and Western masters in consciousness to be a state of arrested development. This samadhi in four yogas illuminates the stages of awareness leading to enlightenment through comparative analysis and progressive meditative exploration. The transformation in consciousness which occurs is nothing less than a mystical encounter with the spirit, relinquishment of the traditional egoic self, and metamorphosis into a flexible, highly adapted man or woman of knowledge and numinous being.

In the final part of Carlos Castaneda's Tales Of Power, don Juan just prior to revealing the sorcerers' explanation to his disciple Carlos, prefaces his discussion with these sage comments:

> *Personal power decides who can or cannot profit by a revelation; my experiences with my fellow men have proven to me that very, very few of them would be willing to listen; and of those few who listen even fewer would be willing to act on what they have listened to; and of those who are willing to act even fewer have enough personal power to profit by their acts.*[10]

This may be the moment of your cubic centimeter of chance!

2. RADICAL SANITY

The Spirit of Enlightenment

There is a saying in psychological circles that you must first become someone, before you can become no one. At first glance this remark seems quite cryptic. After all, aren't all of us someone? And why would anyone want to become no one?

Often, with very little inward exploration, we live our lives entrained in an inner dialog constructed during our youth, a dialog that remains largely unexamined for the rest of our lives. For example when we sense an insult we may reflexively become angry or resentful. Although the insult may have occurred months or years ago we can resurrect it into present awareness in an instant. We may roll it over in our minds long after the incident, wrecking what would otherwise have been fine moments. Our automatic knee-jerk self-importance is always hovering in the background, ready to erupt into emotional flights of fancy at a moment's notice. We yearn to break from these oft-repeated habits and episodes of disruptive thought and behavior, but lacking the tools and discipline, we rarely achieve permanent change in our behavior.

We take for granted that we truly are the person our profession and given name implies. I am reminded of the apocryphal beachside story of a panicked mother beseeching passing bathers, "Help, help, my son, —the doctor, is drowning!" Each of us constructs in consciousness a representation of an egoic-self, and forgets that the representation is self-created. During the Great Depression men jumped from tall buildings, their self-created egoic-being expiring along with their attachment to a no longer existent financial stockpile. He who dies with the most toys "wins", and having lost all toys there is no point in living! Our self-created public image becomes imperative to our sense of well being, and often we would relinquish our health or lives rather than relinquish our imagined public stature or admiration. It would seem that our pets have greater wisdom in this regard. When we are howling in psychic pain often we forget whom it is who is doing the psychic pinching. This all important egoic-self, which is momentarily constructed and reconstructed in consciousness, drives our actions towards an invisible and equally imaginary and unattainable omega point of satisfactory wealth and stature. The egoic-self is rarely if ever sated in its acquisition of material goods, and as soon as one level of accumulation is achieved, the next stage of wanting begins. We rarely, if ever, truly explore the mystery of consciousness, and all too often conclude our lives with both personal and cosmic questions unchallenged and unresolved. In the following chapters we will explore the seed of mastery inherent in consciousness, the path to self-transcendence through inner tranquility and discerning wisdom, and the fruition of enlightenment in this life through emergence of the transcendental Self.

Let us return to the question of the unexamined and unofficially knighted ruler of the inner realm, the egoic-self. The actual inward search for a self is seldom undertaken and it is normally taken for granted that there is a self. Because I see that I appear different from everyone else, and have my own unique place in the world, how can it be that I do not have a self?

Imagine we are viewing a man sitting in the middle of a room. We as the outside observer cannot know precisely what it is that he is thinking. However, assuming he is awake and just sitting, there are a number of assumptions we can make. First of all, he most likely identifies with his given name and occupation, as well as a variety of family and business relationships. He may not consciously be thinking or considering his personal identity, however at some level we can assume that he believes that he totally knows who he is i.e., a salesman, a vice-president, a husband, a doctor, etc. If you ask him, he may respond, "I am professor Jones, head of Anthropology at the University of Chicago." His answer is assured and without hesitation. His world is constructed around his self identity and his social security number, family name, marital relationship, etc. are the apparent proof of this facade concretized in consciousness. Adi Da, a profoundly realized Adept, and innovator of his own school of enlightenment, speaks to us from a position of radical understanding. He comments on the creation of a self in consciousness:

> The conventional activity of the born being is to presume a sense of identity, which presumption is based on the appearance of phenomena. We perceive that there is a body-mind, a physically based self. In our un-

Realized or un-Enlightened state the consciousness that is the field of that very perception conceives of Itself in terms of this bodily presentation. It calls Itself "I" and thinks Itself to be identical with this bodily self. The phenomena in the mental field are likewise interpreted to imply that Consciousness is limited by and identical to the stream of egoic consciousness and thought.[11]

To be born into this plane of existence is to assume an identity, and make this presumption of identity with the patterns of body-mind. Apparent universal consensus keeps us from examining the myths of our particular culture. We can readily see, however, the entrapment created through superstitious beliefs adopted by people not indigenous to our culture. Every individual falls prey to unexamined belief systems, and you and I are not an exception.

Let us begin to examine the proposition of a *self* at the apparent beginning of our physical presence: the sperm and the egg. All organic matter is apparently composed of chemical constituents. Chemicals are derived from atomic matter. Atomic matters arise as time-space fields within the universe. We are a construct of a time-space field. Time-space fields have never been observed. Time-space fields are constructs in consciousness. Does the material world exist independent of a time-space observer, —or is it that consciousness precedes the material world and that the material world arises within and as an aspect of consciousness? Our mind creates elaborate descriptions in consciousness in an attempt to describe and make known to itself a perceived exterior reality. Ultimate reality can neither be described as being interior or exterior to mind, since the mechanism measuring the perceived reality, the mind, arises as a function of the very plane of reality that the mind is attempting to observe. It is as though the eye is attempting to see the eye. A being existing without anything beyond its own boundaries would have no point of reference to gauge itself. A reality without any being would have no means of detecting its own existence.

You, as the assembler and witness of reality, interpret the signals of the five senses in conjunction with the inner dialog as being the *self*. However, if you were to penetratingly examine your inner awareness—you would not find a *self*! And in spite of your not being able to find this elusive *self*, you will, as is typical of people of our time and culture, still insist that there is a *self*. As long as you are bound to perceptions and the inner dialog as being identical to "concrete reality", you are bound by the descriptions of the verbal and sensory mind, and the unexamined belief systems of Western civilization.

Everything we label with arbitrary sounds called words, everything we are taught, believe or can conceive, lies within the definitions created by mind or utilizing the term of the Central American sorcerer and seer don Juan, the tonal. The unknown, or the nagual for don Juan, is the underlying, formless, unimaginable, indescribable ground of all existents. The tonal and the nagual are the two halves of the mystery of being. As we continue our journey in consciousness we will examine the tonal and the nagual in depth, penetrating deeper into the mysterious world revealed by the Central American master of awareness, don Juan.

We come into this life and exist in infancy as all nagual. Our actions, and reactions, are direct, nonverbal, and without constructs of time and space. All that occurs, occurs in the immediate moment. As we acquire language, we lose our sense of direct participation and begin to label events, delay gratification vis-à-vis the construction in language of the future, and the resurrection and con- sideration of no longer existent, or past events. Our tonal fabricates, organizes, and facilitates the passage through this existence in our personally emerging stream of consciousness.

Through acculturation we confuse the menu of language for the meal of being. It is as though the anticipation of future happiness, or recollection of prior success, is more immediate and real than right now. We forget that we have created the inner dialog corresponding to our particular desires, and avoidances. We cling to concepts in consciousness, projected as though they were separate from consciousness. We erect a personal self through the assimilation in consciousness of the five senses and the emerging inner dialog. We incorporate into the self-representation abstractions from parents, teachers, and friends. We gradually lose sight of the other half of ourselves, the balance and knowledge of the silent nagual, the ineffable, mystery of our existence. We become unknowingly, self- pinching victims of the self-created tonal. Our existence is domi- nated by the menu of the tonal through our incessant inner chatter.

We have subjugated our nagual—the meal, the spirit and feeling of being, to the tonal. Don Juan tells his disciple and master chronicler, Carlos Castaneda, that our tonal, that should have been a benevolent guardian, has become a tyrannical despot.

It has always been the goal of spiritual leaders, shamen, yogis, and men of knowledge to assist in balancing the two halves of mankind, — the tonal and the nagual, reason and will, mind and spirit; and in helping the individual to a more sane, spiritually enriched being. The power of meditation is revealed through the practice of stilling the inner dialog. At the union of tranquility and meditative insight we are no longer dominated by our internal dialog and we are free to see things as they are.

When the seeker first awakens from his dreams it is often only a fleeting realization. He may fear that he is losing his sanity. However, he soon realizes he cannot lose that which he never possessed. Adi Da, the creator of a singularly unique, radical[12] nondual (advaityana) Buddhism,[13] lucidly describes the nature of the realization of being the witness in consciousness:

> The Witness-Consciousness is Primarily aware Of and As Itself. It Is (or May Be) secondarily (or Peripherally) Aware of the act of attention and the objects of attention (and The Root Feeling Of Relatedness, Which Is The conditional Origin Of attention), but, Fundamentally, It Stands As Itself, Inherently Sensitive To The Native (or Unconditional) Feeling Of Being, And Basically Indifferent To whatever Arises Conditionally, While Also Freely (or Tacitly) Allowing whatever arises conditionally To Arise and be Noticed.[14]

Free of the internal dialog we can see consciousness as the clear, mirror-like water of being, with mind as the maker of ripples, and occasionally—great waves! Whenever an image arises juxtaposed upon the clear water of consciousness, attention appears to transform the clear water into objects separate from consciousness. Until we transcend this root feeling of relatedness, where we feel attached to the discriminations arising in consciousness, we feel bound by illusions of our own making. Adi Da likens consciousness to a still pond reflecting images and always unchanged:

> To Be The Witness-Consciousness Is to Be Consciousness Itself, Simply Aware Of Itself As that Which Merely and Freely Reflects conditions. Just As The Still Pond Water Reflects the Foolish face of Narcissus,

Motivelessly. Even all kinds of conditions May arise To That Native Awareness, but No Feeling Of Identification With them, or The Search For Them, or The Effort Of Holding On To them, or The Felt Need To Avoid them Is There In the Witness-Consciousness Itself. Indeed, All Motivations Towards action Are themselves Simply Observed (or Merely Reflected) By (and In) The Witness-Consciousness Itself.[15]

Until the meditator resides in and as the still pond, every passing thought carries him along the labyrinths of mind. Like a leaf at the mercy of the wind, he is the vortex of every encounter. He projects that which is immediately apprehended as though it did not arise within. He ascribes motivations and behavior to others—when, in fact, he is merely the witness of discriminations and perceptions within his own consciousness. To be free of this unenlightened trance state will require courage, will, wisdom, and faith. Mark Dyczkowski in his masterful, *The Doctrine of Vibration*, quotes the great mystic Shaivist sage, Abhinavagupta, who defines the activity of mind, reflective awareness:

It is the capacity of the Self to know itself in all its purity in the state of perfect freedom from all kinds of affections, due either to the internal or the external causes; to retain these affectations in the form of residual traces (samskara); to take out at will, at any time, anything out of the existing stock of traces samskaras and bring back an old affected state of itself as in the case of remembrance; to create an altogether new state of self-affection by making a judicious selection from the existing stock and displaying the material so selected on the background of the prakasa aspect as at the time of free imagination.[16]

Mark Dyczkowski considers self-reflective awareness, when freed from all associations, in his gloss of Abhinavagupta's Isvara-pratyabhijna-vimarsini;

Cognition would be impossible if consciousness were incapable of it (reflective awareness). This capacity is the reflective awareness it has of itself as pure `I´ consciousness. When it is conditioned by the object of knowledge, which is in its turn conditioned by the forces and laws that govern the physical universe (all of which are aspects of the power of Maya), it operates as cognition, memory and all the other functions of the mind. Cognition, in other words, is the reflective awareness of `I´ limited by the affections imposed upon it by the variety of external manifestations generated by this `I´ consciousness itself. Freed from all associations with outer objects, the individual shares in God's bliss, which is the experience He enjoys at rest in His own nature. This

*blissful self-awareness (vimarsa) is the abiding condition of the subject
even while he perceives the world and reacts to it. It is the inner activity
of the Spanda principle, which is the inspired wonder (camatkara) of
consciousness from which the power of will, knowledge and action flow
out as phases in its vibrating rhythm (spanda).*[17]

Adi Da discusses a strategy for being of this world, but not in it,
and concludes somewhat humorously:

*Observe The Manner Of My Lifetime (When I Am Physically Alive In
Bodily Human Form). When I Am (Thus) Alive, I Simply Observe and
Allow and Relate To whatever arises and whatever Is Brought To Me. I
Act and Serve Spontaneously and In freedom. I Do Whatever Is
Necessary To Preserve or Promote Relational Harmony, Natural
Equanimity, True and Even Perfect Humor, and Divine Enlightenment.
I Do Not Abandon The Heart-Force Of Inherent Happiness. I See There
Is Only Inherent Happiness, Love-bliss, or Self-Radiance (Rather than
self-Contraction, Un-Happiness, Un-Love, and Non-Bliss). Therefore, I
Do Not Seek. I Am Certain that whatever arises conditionally Is Merely
and Only A Chaos Of limits, changes, and endings. Therefore, I Simply
Persist, Without Illusions. Happiness, or Love-Bliss, Is My Indifference.
Happiness, or Love-Bliss, Is The Only Real Freedom In This Midst.
Therefore, I Let all conditions arise, stay awhile, and pass. I Play My
Given and Expected Roles. So What?* [18]

The Lankavatara Sutra is one of a handful of Buddhist texts that
speak to the reader exclusively from the enlightened point of view.
Thus while the Lankavatara is not a teaching text, and its meaning is
not readily discernible to one who cannot attain meditative absorption, it is useful in that its purity of expression is a benchmark
against which one can measure progress. Adi Da in the Introductory
Comments to the Dwight Goddard compilation of The Lankavatara
Sutra speaks of the unusual difficulty in assimilating the sutra:

*It is a kind of "Catch 22" literature. You know that the Truth is ultimate
transcendence of the discriminative mind, but in order to realize the
transcendence of the discriminative mind, you must have already
realized transcendence of the discriminative mind! Any approach you
might make to it is the exercise of the discriminative mind and therefore
inadequate. Basically the argument in each of the seventh stage texts is
that anything you want to do to realize the Transcendental position is
the exercise of the discriminative mind, and that is precisely what is
wrong with you—you are exercising the discriminative mind.*[19]

On the other hand one begins to acquire a foreign language by just beginning! Let us begin by examining the Buddha's view regarding the four perfections in consciousness:

> Buddha: They are (1) meditation on the lucidity of one's mind, (2) abandonment of (absolute) arising, dwelling, or dissolving, (3) understanding that external reality is without substance, and (4) a deep yearning for discerning awareness.[20]

The Buddha is describing a state of mind that only meditators are normally aware of, the lucidity of one's consciousness. We can become aware of the abiding nature of consciousness during meditation when focused single-pointedly. When words are no longer arcing across the sky of mind a great secret is revealed. Imagine, for a moment, a fish deep in the ocean, lying motionless, suspended in thoughtless gaze. He has no thought of the past or future, his senses expand omni-directionally, reflecting the unity of inner and outer awareness. When a new perception arises he notices it momentarily, and if no action is required, resumes his gaze. Without language to construct likes and dislikes, yesterday and tomorrow, he rests in space-like at-Onement. Like the raven of Jesus, he wants not for the morrow. His consciousness is clear, empty and blisslike. He appears to be in samadhi.

When we are asleep and dreaming, we are entranced by the passing story. Upon awaking we notice that it was only a dream. Until we go to sleep again, we remain entranced by our waking story. To be fully awake and enlightened is to be awake from the trance of the night-dream, as well as the day-dream. You are mistaken if you believe that it is the yogi, or advanced meditator who is in the trance state. Just the opposite is true. Unless you have already awakened, it is you who are in the trance state—entrained in the labyrinths of egoic digression; and it is the yogi who is totally awake. When we abandon the view of (absolute) arising, dwelling, or dissolving, we become aware in consciousness that the past, the present, and the future are wisps of thought construct floating across the screen of mind. Because the mind can never see beyond the mind, the tonal, or verbal self is the creator of time. The nagual, the witness of consciousness, is never functionally attached to apparent changes, arising or dissolving in consciousness, and remains the immutable, formless, and timeless witness of all. If this were not so, where is the past moment? Where is the future moment? Is it not true that this moment of now appears to be continually sliding off the plate of awareness, while you the witness of all are always the same?

This apparent moment of now, constructed in consciousness, can never be experienced by anyone other than you as the witness of consciousness. Your interpretation of this very moment of now can never be consensually validated because you are both the unique witness and creator of this very moment. Just as a dream can never be consensually validated by the apparent participants in the dream (who ultimately are simply aspects of your consciousness), neither can the apparent participants in your waking moment (who ultimately are simply representations in consciousness of apparent others) consensually validate your moment of now. The grosser aspects of this moment of now can be agreed upon by others in proximity to you, however the experience of this moment of now—your sense of what is happening—is non-veridical or illusory. If you attempt to look back at the occurrences of a mere moment ago you will see that you cannot see or resurrect that which never truly occurred. You may say, "Of course it occurred, I just boarded the train!" I would agree that you just boarded the train. We are not attempting to negate conventional reality, no more than we would attempt to persuade you that you did not experience flying through a wall in last evening's dream. Both daytime and dreamtime occurrences are indeed witnessed. It is that both dream and waking moment arise uniquely within your consciousness and are ultimately without consensual validity, duration, or substance! You can show me a book you purchased yesterday, or we can share a cake you baked today, but just try and share with me what you perceived as having occurred a moment ago. There is no moment ago—now—nor future moment—now—there is only, and always, this mysterious, beginingless and endless moment of the feeling of Being!

This very moment of now, erected and witnessed in consciousness, transcends the three periods of time, and is without causation. If consciousness itself were not the most prior subject of subjectivity then consciousness would require an endless regression of prior causation. In other words, for consciousness to occur in and as this apparent universe either consciousness is caused and requires a prior act of creation—or it is not caused and requires no prior act of causation! A prior act of creation requires a still further prior act of creation and finally— and endless series of prior acts of creation of consciousness. This consideration leads us to either requiring an endless regression of prior acts of creation, or an uncaused, infinitely present sense of consciousness itself—a consciousness or Being which simply transcends the three periods of time. Consciousness is the utmost subject of subjectivity. Consciousness is both the witness and creator of apparent reality. Experiencing this we are facing the mysterious nagual. We are *seeing* an external, as well as internal reality without inherent substance. A moment of meditative awareness will clarify the sky of mind.

It is difficult to appropriate discerning awareness. Occasionally we have a fleeting glimpse of the essence of consciousness or the nature of our being. The tonal may loosen its grip when we are deeply in love and egoic boundaries are dissolved. When we surrender to love we utilize previously dormant aspects of feeling to construct our world. When we gaze into the eyes of our loved one, our internal dialogue quiets down, and the feeling of love transcends our egoic self. Our thoughts of money, taxes, and death are relinquished. We yearn for this heightened sense of pleasure and release from inner chatter. We do not believe that we can transfer this wellness of being and love to our daily life. And as long as we do not appropriate a discerning awareness to clarify and transform the sky of mind, we will shuttle between the tonal and the nagual, entranced by both. The struggle of the warrior is to balance the two halves of himself, the tonal and the nagual. The warrior only witnessing, never clinging, never attached, effortlessly resides in his samadhi of being and love. He is the giver of knowledge, not the keeper; he is the source of love, not the seeker. When he has a partner he loves; when he has no partner he loves. He is the source, the wellspring of love and knowledge, no longer dependent on others for his inexhaustible supply of compassion, forgiveness, patience, and wisdom.

Examining Love

If we have repeatedly made and lost friends, dated endlessly, or married often and unsatisfactorily, how many lessons do we require before we come to know that we must first love ourselves, before we can join in love with someone else. Certainly there are people who are attractive enough in appearance, but not at the right stage of personal growth for our consideration as friend or lover. When we become involved with people for their appearance and because of our need to present a certain kind of appearance to the world, rather than from deep friendship and love, inevitably we swing from relationship to relationship, as a monkey swings from vine to vine, not releasing the first relationship before we grasp the next. When our love for ourselves is not fulfilled, we come to meet or acquire friends and lovers from a place of need, rather than a place of wholeness and well-being. Not unexpectedly, body and thought are synchronized in neurotic reactivity. Not until we are totally at one with ourselves when alone for extended periods of time, will we be in a position to become friends with people having mutual interests, rather than mutual neediness. When we become the source of our own love, not dependent on parents, or lovers, or material possessions, we will be the limitless source of unconditional happiness.

The path to self-love is through spiritual development, and transcending the neurotic mind. Spiritual development comes about through the vanquishing of the neurotic mind. Meditation is the practice of spiritual development. Meditation is a method for the exploration of consciousness through simultaneous mindfulness and analysis of consciousness. The goal of this exploration is a stabilization and mastery of awareness, transcendence of the ego, and the beginning of spiritual awakening. Spiritual awakening is accompanied by nondual awareness, love, compassion, and understanding. Nondual awareness is the state in which we all live, however, usually occluded for most of us by projections within consciousness. Nondual awareness occurs when we no longer divide our consciousness into subject and object, and perceive inner projections as outer reality. Nondual awareness eliminates our playing victim to our own illusions. Meditation is the means of awakening from the nightmare of self-inflicted shadow projections. It is the means of self-empowerment, self-love, and radical happiness. Love is not to be conceptualized, but to be surrendered to at the heart. It is not true that you need a sex partner to experience love. Love is always experienced from within, in consciousness. One's loved one, most often, is the vehicle to trigger the love feeling, but in truth, without an inner surrendering to no-thought, to pure bliss-like emotional feeling in consciousness, love is only a conception in words, and is not powerfully appropriated in experience.

Adi Da – The Wound Of Love

The most valued skills are acquired through unrelenting practice. The accomplishment of ecstatic, selfless love is acquired in the perfection of samadhi. When we say, "I love you", often we are delivering words, empty of the feeling-experience. When we forget feeling, we confuse our symbols for the objects themselves. I am reminded of the Zen comment of mistaking the finger pointing at the moon, for the moon. Saying, "I love you", is not necessarily experiencing love. I am not referring to love in the conventional sense. I am signifying a love, having been experienced with willful volition as a consequence of the power within to set aside the ordinary world of commerce and thought, into the mystical experience and feeling of loving. Not only for the sake of loving, but paralleled by the ability to set aside the hypnotic pull of everyday life, and surrender with power into the wordless samadhi of playing, laughing and loving.

When others reject us, the tendency to become un-love must be transcended. While others may at times be bereft of love, to match their lack of love is counter-productive, strategically without wisdom, and ultimately we deprive ourselves of love. Adi Da explains:

...You must Also Constantly Encounter, Understand, and Transcend the Rejection Rituals Of others who Are, Even If Temporarily or Only Apparently, Bereft Of Divine Wisdom. Therefore, If You Will Be Love (As My Devotee, and Thus and Thereby, As A Devotee Of The Divine Person), You Must (In the Way and Manner Of The Heart) Always Skillfully Transcend The Tendency To Become Un-Love (and Thus To Become self-Bound, Apparently Divorced From Grace-Given Divine Communion) In Reaction To the Apparent Lovelessness Of others. And You Must Not Withdraw From Grace-Given Divine Communion (or Become Degraded By Un-Love) Even When Circumstances Within Your Intimate Sphere, or Within The Sphere Of Your Appropriate social Responsibility, Require You To Make Difficult Gestures To Counter and Control The Effects or Undermine and Discipline The Negative and

Destructive Effectiveness Of the Rituals Of Un-Love That Are Performed By others.[21]

Adi Da notes that it is neither possible, nor necessary to overcome the feelings of rejection. He suggests that nothing less than being Love itself is called for, rather than always being at the effect of waiting to receive Love:

> *If You Will Do this, Then You Must Do the Sadhana (or Concentrated Practice) Of Love. As A Practical Matter, You Must Stop Dramatizing the egoic Ritual Of Betrayal In Reaction To The Feeling Of Being Rejected. You Must Understand, Transcend, and Release The Tendency To Respond (or React) To Signs Of Rejection (or Signs That You Are Not Loved) As If You Are Insulted, Rather Than Wounded. That Is To Say, You Must Stop Punishing and Rejecting others When You Feel Rejected. If You Punish another When You Feel This, You Will Act As If You Are Immune To Love's Wound. Thus, You Will Pretend To Be Angrily Insulted, Rather Than To Suffer To Be Wounded. In the Process, You Will Withdraw and Withhold Love. You Will Stand Off, Independent and Dissociated. You Will Compound It By Actually Rejecting the other. In This Manner, You Will Become Un-Love. You Will Fail to Love. You Will Fail To Live In the Sphere Of Love. Your Own Acts Of Un-Love Will Degrade You, Delude You, and Separate You From Your Love-partner (or Your partners In Love) and From Love Itself. Therefore, those who Fail To Practice The Sadhana Of Love In their intimate emotional-sexual relationships, and In human relationships Generally, Will, By That Failure Turn Away (or Contract) From God (or The Great Condition That Is Reality Itself).*[22]

Adi Da points out that loving beings are loved, and that others eventually, or inevitably love them. In the search for love from others, we give up our already established position of love, lose the knowing-feeling of love, and then pursue others for that which we already possess. To be the incarnation of love itself is ultimately more satisfying, spiritually enriching, and self-empowering than the search for love. Observe children in moments of profound peace. They live in the moment, their eyes shine deeply with luminescent love and laughter. As children acquire language and desire, ambition and greed, their eyes lose that shine. Having grown up, our eyes have also lost that shine. It is within our grasp to re-ignite that luminosity. In order to rekindle our inner glow, we must surrender artfully and with ease, to wordless, empowered loving.

Ludwig Wittgenstein, possibly the twentieth century's most renowned philosopher, said *you must use words to reach a higher understanding—but ultimately words are meaningless. After having climbed the ladder of words, you must drop them to know a higher understanding.* Words are merely aids along the path to achieve this higher understanding. Words must be dropped in order to bring the mind to tranquility. The tranquil mind is one that is in union with silence. There is absolute stillness. Thoughts occasionally arise from within the void of consciousness, as clouds drifting across a desert sky. One's consciousness drifts to the place of witnessing, rather then into labyrinth-like tunnels of thought. The discursive process comes to a complete halt, and you are aware of the apparent place, dimension, time, and the feeling of being arising in consciousness. You are not in some altered state of reality. You are naked awareness, devoid of dualistic presence. You see that you are not looking out at the world, and that the world is neither internal nor external, but arising in consciousness.

The practice of the dissolution of egoic boundaries, meditative absorption, and the acquisition of discerning awareness may be complemented by exceedingly fine incense, such as, Avabhasa (The "Bright") Rose Incense.[23] Marvelously fragrant and subtle aromas facilitate quieting the mind by shifting attention into exotic and pungent rapture. The hypnotic strains of Brian Eno's superlative music, "Thursday Afternoon"[24], may further ease the surrender of mind-chatter into single-pointed clarity, emptiness, and bliss. The songs of the enlightened masters of the Mahamudra, and the divine poetry of Adi Da facilitate the mastery of the one flavor samadhi of love-bliss. Ultimately, however, entrancing music and sensory invoking incense are temporary devices that may be set aside as the mastery of consciousness stabilizes. What is required is the ability to become profoundly aware of sensory input and enable the shift away from the internal dialogue. Finally, both sensory input and the internal dialog are to be transcended in single-pointed awareness. Je Phagdru describes the dawning of meditative absorption:

When one-pointed absorption first dawns in one's stream-
  consciousness,

Its serenity and lucidity is beyond description.
It is clear and without any substance, like space.[25]

The material world does not precede consciousness, for if it did, who would be there to perceive it? And without perception, how or why would the world exist? In the still of the quiet mind it is revealed that the world, body and mind, arise in consciousness. The theater of mind is phantasmagorically rich, paradoxically empty, and arises and dissolves in consciousness. Transcending the discursive mind is the pathway to the feeling of love.

Examining Consciousness

Sleeping, I accept all that arises as real, later to awaken and know my dream arose as an illusion in consciousness. If I awoke within my dream and were aware that I was dreaming, I might be able to consider my everyday waking world. From the vantage point of the lucid dreamer, how would I observe the dreamer's dream, and the waking life? From the position of being awake in the middle of a dream, would my daily life appear as a dream as well? Awake, I know all that arises as reality arises in consciousness as a non-binding modification of consciousness. If all that arose were binding, there could be no apparent movement of life's story. This apparent moment of now would be frozen in consciousness for eternity! Finally, I see that I am the play of consciousness—momentary, trans-lucent, and mysterious. Examining consciousness, I see that con-sciousness transcends beginning and end, and is without form, shape, or color. The body-mind arises in consciousness, along with the apparent world. The mystery to be explored in meditation is the very nature, essence and foundation of consciousness.

Much has been written about Buddhism's so-called negation of reality. Negation is not the way of Buddhism. The Buddhist way is just one way among many, such as the teachings of Christ, the Hindu theology, the teachings of Don Juan, and countless others pointing towards awaking from the tyranny of self into a higher realm of being—the transcendental self or the enlightened one. The Buddhist path is one among many paths teaching the practice of enlightenment, the mastery of self, the divinity of awareness, and the actualization of the realized being in the world as it is. It is not that

Jesus or Buddha or don Juan negate the conventional world in nihilistic destruction, rather they proselytize the world to awaken to spiritual wholeness, wellness, and never ending growth and challenge within and beyond the realm of ordinary human potential.

The potential of this plane of awareness is transcendence of the apparent reality arising in consciousness. Struggle is a key feature; for to be ultimately, finally and absolutely without struggle would mean that one were either in absolute bliss or absolute nothingness. If we were born in absolute bliss then there would never be any need to experience space or time, because all of our needs would be at one with us. All would be immediately, and forever satisfied. If we were in absolute nothingness, there could never be an apparent requirement or experience or beginning or end. This moment, this birth, this being, is the necessary prerequisite for experience, and apparent separation from and absolute union with God. Without this struggle, this paradox of apparent separation from, and union with God, there would be only the void. But to believe substantively in the struggle—or the void, is to be asleep.

The lioness in the field hunts to survive. Often she goes for days without food. She appears not to sulk between successes. An eagle soars across a trackless sky, ever in the present, ever alert, fulfilling its destiny. Only man has the potential to construct vast and complex relations in mind, and then succumb to his self made myth of ultimate happiness in material attainment. Only man has the ability to set aside false constructs, and fulfill a greater destiny. Fulfillment, culminating in the light of enlightenment, is the next stage in human development. Every human being is born with the potential for enlightenment. In a parable from Jesus of Nazareth, when the tiniest of seeds dissolves in fertile soil there is a transformation of being into the kingdom of heaven:

> The disciples said to Jesus, "Tell us what the kingdom of heaven is like."
> He said to them, "It is like a mustard seed, the tiniest of all seeds. But when it falls on prepared soil, it grows into a large plant and shelters the birds of the sky." [26]

The continual, repetitive and self-deluding inner chatter must dissolve in consciousness in order to access the kingdom of heaven. There is no ultimate savior, organization, belief system or magic that will lead us to sanity, spiritual growth, and the practice of divine love. Ultimate sanity and salvation develop from a seed within consciousness. This seed has been planted within fertile soil, but as is so often true within nature, only a few will survive and grow. Unlike the seed within nature, however, through our own volition we can nurture our inner seed to flower with enlightenment. The inner seed is the guru, consciousness is the path, and the practice is the union of tranquility, love, and wisdom. The rest is up to you. Choose wisely.

Search For Sanity

Shortly after I pondered Zeno's paradox in a very fine book, *The Promise of Scientific Humanism*, (unfortunately out of print for many years) I began to change my view of the world. Zeno, a Greek philosopher, said that in order to have motion—a thing must move from where it is, to where it is not. Since a thing clearly cannot be where it is not, motion is impossible. In struggling to understand Zeno's paradox it is useful to consider how we use words to describe apparent reality. Zeno, without defining motion, leads us to the conclusion that motion is impossible. Our use of words precludes anything other than either a yes or no, motion or no motion, hot or cold, white or black, etc. Early physicists discuss motion as being intrinsically tied to time and space. Albert Einstein went further and said that there is no such thing as a separate time and a separate space; there is only time-space. Had Zeno been aware of Einstein's postulate he might have rephrased his paradox to say, 'In order to have absolute stability, or motionlessness, there must be no time-space. Since time-space pervades all, a lack of motion is impossible.' A Buddhist, or don Juan might say that neither interpretation is quite right. Motion, is merely a non-binding modification in consciousness. Don Juan considers the nature of consciousness:

> *"Man doesn't move between good and evil," he said in hilariously rhetorical tone, grabbing the salt and pepper shakers in both hands. "His true movement is between negativeness and positiveness."*
> *He dropped the salt and pepper and clutched a knife and fork.*
> *"You're wrong! There is no movement, he continued as if he were answering himself. Man is only mind!"* [27]

The Great Master [Milarepa] sang:[28]

This mental consciousness — the inner movement —
Is the source of karma and mental defilements;
It remains ignorant as long as it lacks understanding,
Yet, when understanding dawns, it becomes self-comprehending
awareness
And the source of virtues.[29]

Words are representations constructed in consciousness in an attempt to impose order on perceptions, and not some immutable sound represented reality. For instance when we say the word chocolate, the sound is only a representation in consciousness of chocolate, and not the substance itself. Various languages represent chocolate with different sound units, with no one language having priority, and neither the sound nor the spelling are an inherent aspect of the substance chocolate. The experience of chocolate is assembled by the senses in union with appearance and emptiness. The experience is empty because it cannot be ascertained that that which is assembled in consciousness is identical with the object from its own side.

All of our representations occur within a closed system of perceptions received and interpreted by the senses. Waves of bounced radiation from the world of external objects are received, analyzed and reconstructed by consciousness. After this process is repeated innumerable times, consciousness forgets that these reconstructed reflected waves are not the external objects themselves! In a relative sense we can perceive the external world; in the ultimate sense we cannot know exactly what the external world is. This is significant because we live in a word constructed world. Our pointers to 'reality' are merely relative, not ultimate, and thus representations are uniquely individual. As Milarepa sang, "...the source of karma and mental defilements."

Another example might be to consider that a tree does not exist within itself in the way that we view tree. The roots of a tree branch beneath the surface of the earth, mixed inseparably with the soil nutrients and moisture. The leaves of the tree are photo-chemically tied to the atmosphere and sun. If we were to map out the entire organism we call "tree", the map would have to include the entire cosmos. In whatever way a tree is organized, it is certainly not organized in any way from the tree's side, or experientially from our side, that we and the tree can share. To be a tree is eternally beyond our knowing.

At this point, if we consider that we are surrounded by a sea of self-named objects through which we define our reality and ourselves, we may see that our words are symbols for a mind made reality. If we can see that there is not a verifiable exterior reality, we may begin to see that our belief in the interior self of consciousness is similarly in jeopardy. For if all of our symbols are only shadows of an unknowable reality, then just what is this self that is viewing this mysterious life, and who, and where are we?

Ken Wilber – The Primary Dualism

It is appropriate to introduce Ken Wilber here. In his extraordinary compilation of Eastern thought and Western psychology, *The Spectrum of Consciousness*, Ken Wilber discusses the nature of human identity and psychological well being in consciousness with penetrating brilliance. He expands upon the Primary Dualism, the illusion in consciousness of a separation between the idea or subject in mind, and the object or field perceived in consciousness:

> *To better understand the Primary Dualism and its creative power of maya [illusion], a simple illustration might help. Let the blank space below represent Mind or the non-dual Void.*[30]

> *This blank space does not mean that the mind is a featureless nothingness — it is only a representation of the fact that Reality is non-conceptual, non-dual, non-objective, etc. Now let us superimpose conceptualization upon this Void by placing a grid 'over' it, as follows:*

Upon the 'blankness' of the Void we have traced several distinctions represented by the crossed lines of the grid. Thus this grid itself represents Logos, word-and-thought, symbolic elaboration, superimposition, dismemberment, maya, dualism, measurement, conceptualization, maps—everything implied in the word 'thought,' since it is by thought, the dualistic mode of knowing, that we fabricate these distinctions, and 'dismember him daily.'

But notice what has happened, the 'unity' (strictly, the 'non-duality') that underlies the grid is no longer directly visible; it has become obscured—the distinctions of the grid have 'split' the underlying unity, and this unity then becomes unnoticed, implicit, unexpressed and thus repressed. This underlying unity now 'appears' or 'manifests' itself or 'projects' itself as a world of 'separate' objects extended in space and time. In the figure, these 'objects,' are represented by the squares of the grid, each of which has boundaries or distinctions that set it apart from the other 'square-things.' The underlying unity, in other words, is now projected as a multiplicity of separate 'things.' Thus dualism, to the extent that we forget its 'underlying ground' of non-duality, represses that non-duality, and then projects it as a multiplicity. Dualism-Repression-Projection: this is the threefold process of maya.

If from the moment of conception prior to birth, to this very moment, we could view our own consciousness with time-lapse photography, we would see, at first, undifferentiated consciousness, and then a blossoming into the consciousness of a typical adult. We have all experienced this growth in consciousness, but nearly all of the non-verbal information has been forgotten or repressed. However, we can imagine that an infant does not have a clearly differentiated sense of the separation of himself from his surroundings. Since he has not yet begun the verbalization process, and the labeling of objects within his field of view and contact, he has no means to define and construct, and differentiate subject and object in consciousness. He and his surroundings are undifferentiated, and one and the same in consciousness. Progressively, as he matures, and his parents and teachers assist him in the labeling process, he begins to form the perception of a separation between himself and the field of objects in his environment.

We, as humans, normally do not construct a conscious presence of air and gravity. Consider, for example, that a fish in water is unlikely to construct a presence of water. It is apparent, however, that the medium in which any organism lives is intrinsic, and vital to the survival of the organism. Generally, separation of the environment from the organism leads to its death. Because we do not perceive certain aspects of our environment does not mean they do not exist. It may only mean that there is usually such a plenitude of the environmental element that the organism does not have to concern itself with the availability of the element. The human organism cannot exist for long without air, gravity, light, suitable environmental temperature range, etc. It is commonly assumed that the human organism is in some profound and exact manner existing separate from these basic requirements. From the point of view of consciousness, the environment or field, and consciousness—are contiguous (arising in nondual union of appearance and emptiness; or arising within the utmost subject of subjectivity—the feeling of Being).

Adi Da – Self-Radiant Consciousness

Man appears to be a conflux of body and mind. On closer examination man exists within a field of sunlight, gravity, earth, atmospheric gases, temperature, etc. Organic and inorganic nutrients are ingested, assimilated—assisted by various bacterial and chemical mediators of digestion and absorption—and either utilized or eliminated. Sunlight bathes man and his environment and various elements are synthesized. Man is not an independent, isolated organism. He cannot and does not exist separate or separated from his environment, and it is impossible to determine where man ends and the environment begins. A more acute way of viewing man would be to say that man is an apparently singular, uniquely configured field structure within a greater surrounding field. Man and his environment appear to exist within a field continuum of atomic structure, composed of varying densities of molecular matter. Atomic structure is a concept developed by man's mind. Ultimately, the mind and all of its concepts, including the body—arise in consciousness. Adi Da discusses body and mind:

> *The body is Not A Someone. There Is no body in itself. The body Depends On mind and Self-Existing (and Self-Radiant) Consciousness*

For all its acts, or Else it Is Nothing More Than a vegetative mass of bonded cells, Dependent On the grosser environment For its substance, and Not Otherwise Differentiated From The Seemingly Infinite Mass Of Grazing cells or atoms Linked In The Organic Chain Of Space. (And Even Space Itself, It Must Be Realized, Is Only Self-Existing and Self-Radiant Consciousness Itself)

The mind Is Not A Someone. There Is no mind in itself. The mind Depends On Self-Existing (and Self-Radiant) Consciousness For all its content (or Significance), or Else it Is Not Even a possibility. There Cannot Be conditional subjectivity (or mind) Without The Perfect Subject (or Inherently Perfect Subjectivity, Which Is Consciousness Itself). Therefore, Without Consciousness, no body Would Be Differentiated In Space (For What Would Be The Purpose?).[31]

If we could view the surface of man at the atomic level we would expect to see complex molecules composed of atoms. If we could go still further and view the atoms we would expect to see protons, electrons, positrons, neutrons, etc. If we could go still further and attempt to define these spinning electrons, we encounter a very strange situation. In 1927, Werner Heisenberg, atomic physicist and author of the Uncertainty Principle, found that if he attempted to measure an atomic particle's position precisely, he could not precisely measure the particle's momentum. If he attempted to measure the particle's momentum precisely, he found he could not precisely measure the particle's position. The physicist's only means of seeing the particle—bombarding it with a single unit of light, the photon—changes the particles location. Unexpectedly, the momentum and position of a particle, as well as the apparent physical universe, are somehow tied to the observer! Werner Heisenberg had unknowingly rediscovered Nagarjuna's centuries old "discerning wisdom" —the union of appearance and emptiness!

Apparent reality is stated to be empty;
Emptiness means apparent reality,
For their mutual nonexclusion is a certainty,
Like the inter relatedness between the conditioned and their
*   transitory nature.[32]*

When we attempt to pin down the nature of the atom we seem to be interacting with an elusive substance that is always one step ahead of the observer. In fact, the particle, according to quantum mechanics, is inseparable from the system, or person attempting to interact with or measure it. The particle does not seem to have attributes that are clearly independent of the observer, or system attempting to make the measurement. There appears to be no clear-cut distinction between the subject of observation and the observer himself! This strange state of subject-object unity was explored in the ancient kingdom of Kashmir, where we will next turn our attention.

3. THE HEART

The Kingdom Of Kashmir

Kashmir is situated high in the North Indian Himalayas and bordered on the north by China, on the west by Pakistan, and on the east by Tibet. This ancient Shangri-La, with deep blue lakes and sparkling rivers, is set five thousand feet above sea level. The lush and fertile valley of Kashmir has been a center of learning for both Hindus and Buddhists. During the tenth century Kashmiris excelled in the study of medicine, astronomy, mathematics, and religion. Studies were conducted in the ancient, and it is said, divinely inspired language, Sanskrit.

Caravans and trade routes criss-crossed this Mecca of learning, and Buddhism spread throughout Central Asia. Many sages came to study in Kashmir to learn Sanskrit in order to translate and unravel the great Buddhist scriptures. Tibetan Buddhist scholars studied and imported the teachings in the seventh century, guided by the first king of Tibet. The Kashmiri Shaivite school flourished under the tutelage of one of the greatest spiritual and mystic geniuses that India ever produced, Abhinavagupta.

Abhinavagupta – The Heart Of Bhairava

The Heart as a metaphor illuminating the nature of consciousness plays an important role in both Kashmir Shaivism and the Advaitayana Buddhism of Adi Da. Let us have our first glimpse of the heart metaphor through the eyes of Abhinavagupta:

The Heart, says Abhinavagupta, is the very Self of Siva, of Bhairava, of the Devi,[33] the Goddess who is inseparable from Siva. Indeed, the Heart is the site of their union (yamala), of their embrace (samghatta). This abode is pure consciousness (caitanya) as well as unlimited bliss (ananda). As consciousness the Heart is the unbounded, infinite light (prakasa) as well as the freedom (svatantrya) and spontaneity (vimarsa) of that light to appear in a multitude and variety of forms. The Heart, says Abhinavagupta, is the sacred fire-pit of Bhairava.[34]

Adi Da – The Way Of The Heart

Adi Da describes the heart as the waking, sleeping and subtle states of consciousness, as well as the state of deep sleep. He affirms that the heart is synonymous with The Divine Being:

> *The heart is the seat of the three conventional states of egoic awareness: the waking state, associated with the left side of the physical heart; the state of dreaming and subtle awareness, associated with the middle or psychic heart; and the state of deep sleep, associated with the root of consciousness and egoity on the right side of the heart, corresponding to the sinoatrial node. These three states correspond to those described in the Eastern esoteric traditions as the gross (waking), subtle (dreaming), and causal (sleeping) states of conscious awareness.*

> *The Heart is God the Divine Self, the Divine Reality. The Realization of the Heart is fully Conscious Awakening as the Self-Existing and Self-Radiant Transcendental, and Inherently Spiritual Divine Being and Person.*
>
> *Divine Self-Realization is associated with the opening of the primal psycho-physical seat of Consciousness and attention in the right side of the heart. Hence the term "the Heart" for the Divine Self. One who is Awake as Consciousness (even in the Witness-Position) generally becomes sensitive to the Current of Spiritual Energy associated with that location in the chest, and he or she feels the mind, or attention, falling into its point of origin there.[35]*

Heart-Master Da distinguishes the Heart as the ultimate Reality from all the psycho-physiological functions of the organic, bodily heart, as well as from the subtle heart, traditionally known as the heart or anahata chakra. The Heart is not "in" the right side of the human heart, nor is it in or limited to the human heart as a whole, or to the body-mind, or to the world. Rather, the human heart and body-mind and the world exist in the Heart, the Divine Being.[36]

A seminal point of examination and understanding for the meditator is whether consciousness is contained within the body, or the body-mind arises in consciousness. The traditional point of view is that your existence is predicated on the body. Without body there is no brain, and ergo no being. At death the animation of the body ceases, and it is commonly believed, so do you. Furthermore, the traditional point of view asserts that the omnipotent, omniscient Creator stands aside, mysteriously involved, eternally unseen, and paradoxically omnipresent.

From the point of view of the meditator reality does not arise independent of consciousness. The bright light of consciousness does not arise within the body or mind. The body-mind and apparent world arise within consciousness. It is not that you as the egoic person are suspended in time and space apart from the divine, or God as some sort of miraculous, but separate, non-spiritual, animated conglomeration of physical matter. It is not that you are merely viewing the world; you are being the world, as well. When discursive reasoning comes to an absolute standstill and awareness no longer moves from the well of infinite stillness, you will experience for yourself the nature of the truth of your own being. That which is witnessed is the subjective point of view projected as though it were outside of, or beyond the consciousness of the viewer, or witness of consciousness. When consciousness no longer divides itself into apparent subject and object, consciousness resides as the witness of apparent reality. You as the witness of consciousness never really capture reality unmediated by your particular perceptive apparatus and beyond the confines of your unique vantage point. What is erected within the confines of the skull and consciousness is perceived and witnessed within consciousness as both internal and external reality. Next we will examine the nondual consciousness school of Kashmir Shaivism, and explore the means whereby consciousness erects self and world, and the nature and identity of consciousness itself.

Kashmir Shaivism – Thirty Six Elements

Let us examine the idea of heart as a representation of "self" in light of the Kashmir Shaivist tradition. In Shaivism the nature of consciousness, and the structuring of a "self" within consciousness, is divided into thirty six elements or *tattvas*. The elements are grouped into seven classifications. The idea here is not to memorize the information we are discussing, just to consider:

The grossest elements of which consciousness is aware are the Five Great Elements: earth, water, fire, air, and ether.

Consciousness is able to differentiate *earth, water, fire,* and *air. Ether* is not perceptible, and is the element within which the activity or occurrence of the other elements occur. You might liken it to the space set aside for the other elements to manifest. It is said in Shaivism that the entire manifestation of the universe is based on these five gross elements.

The next higher elements in consciousness are the Five Subtle Elements: *smell, taste, form, touch, sound.*

The sensation of *smell* arises from earth. The sensation of *taste* arises from water. The impression of *form* arises from *fire.* The sensation of *touch* arises from air. Lastly, *sound* arises from *ether.*

The next higher elements in consciousness are the Five Organs of Action: *creative, excretion, foot, hand, and speech.*

These elements in consciousness are all based upon the preceding elements and are the elements with which we interact with the physical world.

The Five Organs of Cognition are still higher in consciousness: *nose, tongue, eye, skin,* and *ear.* [37]

Now we are not only describing the physical organs of *nose, tongue, eye, skin,* and *ear,* we are pointing towards the experience in consciousness produced when these Five Organs of Cognition interact with the environment. *Nose* creates *smell.* Tongue creates *taste* or *flavors. Eye* creates *form within consciousness. Skin* creates a *feeling of touch. Ear* creates the *sensation of sound.*

All of these twenty elements are viewed by the Shaivists as objective elements. That is because, as they occur, awareness moves away from absolute subjectivity, suppressing for a moment the awareness of the subjective self. Awareness then focuses upon one of these twenty elements, and projects the element or combination of elements in consciousness. During the initial act of perception the *Spandakarikavivrti* describes three stages:

1) The initial outpouring of sensory activity. This phase corresponds to the initial unfolding of the senses towards their object when they 'face' it and the subject is intent on its perception.

2) The initial phase intensified or stabilized. At this stage the senses are actively affected by their object which they now clearly perceive and which abides at one with their field of awareness.

3) When their operation reaches a fruitful conclusion, the object is abandoned and sensory activity merges with the undifferentiated awareness of pure consciousness.[38]

The advanced meditator, or yogi, remains firmly at the center of his field of awareness, noticing *the moment-to-moment creation, persistence and destruction of the universe* (bhairava) formed within the five senses. Ksemaraja, in his *Vijnanabhairava* instructs the yogi in the means of remaining at the now luminous center:

If you project the vision and all the other powers of the senses simultaneously everywhere onto their respective objects by the power of awareness, while remaining firmly established in the center like a pillar of gold, you will shine as the One, the foundation of the universe.[39]

Mark Dyczkowski – Shiva and Shakti

Mark Dyczkowski, a brilliant scholar and yogi in the Kashmir Shaivist tradition discusses the sambhavapaya, or Divine Means of direct realization:

The yogi who recognizes that pure consciousness, free of thought-constructs (nirvikalpa), is his basic state, can practice in any way he chooses; even the most common Mantra will lead him directly to the highest state. Thus the forms of contemplative absorption, empowered (sakta) and the individual state (anava) that are the fruits of the other means to realization both attain maturity in this same undifferentiated awareness. This awareness is the pure ego manifest at the initial moment of perception (prathamikalocana), when the power of the will to perceive is activated. It is the subtle state of consciousness that reveals the presence and nature of its object directly:[40]

That which shines and is directly grasped in the first moment of perception while it is still free of differentiated representations and reflects upon itself is [the basis of the Divine Means] said to be the will. Just as an object appears directly to one whose eyes are open without the intervention of any mental cogitation (anusamdhana), so, for some, does Siva's nature.[41]

Abhinavagupta reveals how physical reality is an aspect of consciousness itself:

The existence or non-existence of phenomena within the domain of the empirical (iha) cannot be established unless they rest within consciousness. In fact, phenomena which rest within consciousness are apparent (prakasamana). And the fact of their appearing is itself their oneness (abheda) with consciousness, because consciousness is nothing but the fact of appearing (prakasa). If one were to say that phenomena were separate from consciousness, and that phenomena appeared, it would be tantamount to saying that "blue" is separate from its own nature. However, one says: "this is blue". Thus, in this sense, phenomena rest in consciousness; they are not separate from consciousness.[42]

Implicit in Abhinavagupta's discourse is the concept that consciousness precedes matter. The implication of this idea is matter shattering! For mind to precede matter, the world of material objects cannot exist as veridical entities. In what sense could matter have form, texture, weight, color, etc., without sensory observation? If absolutely no consciousness existed in the universe, what would be the purpose of matter? For what purpose would matter be differentiated in time and space? How would time and space be differentiated? When these questions are explored as a matter of philosophical inquiry, the answers remain locked in verbiage. When these questions are explored in consciousness absorbed in meditation, the answers become a directly experienced certainty. Stopping the internal dialog and settling the mind in tranquility is the first step in appropriating higher understanding. Examining the nature of tranquil mind, Abhinavagupta speaks of the power of Siva to manifest through the medium of consciousness, the manifest play of forms that we perceive as reality:

Siva in effect is nothing more than this consciousness, which unfolds itself everywhere in the form of a great light. Its very conditions as Siva consists in the fact that all the varied forms of the universe appear. This process of manifestation into all the forms of the universe produces itself completely freely within him.[43]

One may liken consciousness to a liquid filled Christmas ball, which when shaken creates a snow scene. The clear liquid is the never changing backdrop, or essence, upon which the transient snow scene unfolds. Consciousness, like the liquid, is an always clear, empty essence in which reality unfolds. Like the surface of a mirror, which while reflecting everything is unchanged, consciousness is the confluence of Siva and Shakti. Shakti is the manifest play of consciousness upon the unstained, immutable co-creator, Siva.

Hua-Yen Buddhism – The Stainless Mirror

In his superlative translations and commentary to the school of Hua-Yen Buddhism, *Entry Into The Inconceivable,* Thomas Cleary relates how Fa-tsang, the third patriarch of Hua-Yen Buddhism likens the essence of mind to a mirror. The real nature, *the essence of mind,* becomes attached to the objects of its own creation:

For example, though the real nature, going along with conditions, becomes defiled or impure, it never loses its inherent purity—that is indeed why it can become defiled or pure according to conditions. This purity is likened to a clear mirror reflecting the defiled and pure while never losing the clarity of the mirror—indeed it is precisely because the mirror does not lose its clarity that it can reflect defiled and pure forms. By the reflection of the defiled and pure forms, in fact, we can know that the mirror itself is pure. So it is, Fa-tsang explains, with the principle of true thusness: it not only becomes defiled and pure without affecting its inherent purity but by its becoming defiled or pure its inherent purity is revealed. Not only does it reveal its inherent purity without obliterating defilement and purity; it is precisely because of its inherent purity that it can become defiled and pure. Here "inherent purity" means emptiness of inherently fixed nature whereas relative "defilement" and "purity" depends on action and the experiencing mind. All mundane and holy states are manifestations of "thusness", yet the essential nature of thusness—which is naturalness—is not affected.

Fa-tsang continues: "Observe that all things are born from causes and conditions, and so have no individual reality, and hence are ultimately empty. Ultimate emptiness is called transcendent wisdom."

In his "Hundred Gates of Ocean of Meanings", Fa-tsang says that "data are not themselves objects—they must depend on the mind; mind is not of itself mind—it must depend on an object. Because they are interdependent, there is no definite origination in the objective realm." [44]

Siva – The Lord Of Dance

An accomplished French yoginî, Lilian Silburn, poetically paints the dance of Shiva, from the tantra of Kashmir Shaivism:

Siva, the sole essence of all that exists, is also the Lord of dance (nataraja). With one of his many hands he holds the drum, the sound vibrations of which give rise to the universe as they generate time and space; with another hand he brandishes the fire of resorption. The movement of the dance conceals his essence, as it whirls about him the flames of the manifestation, while the fire of resorption, sweeping away everything, reveals it. Standing still at the center of this twofold activity, as the seat of all power, he unfolds, with impassability, the fiercest energies, the most antagonistic movements: emanation and resorption, concealment and grace, reaction and expansion.[45]

Mark Dyczkowski tells us how the universal dance unfolds, "Free of all hopes and fears the enlightened yogi sees all things as part of this eternal cosmic game, played in harmony with the blissful rhythm of his own sportive nature at one with things." *The Stanzas of Vibration* teach:

Everything arises out of the individual soul and he is in all things. Being aware of them, he perceives his identity with them. Therefore there is no state in the thought of words or their meanings that is not Siva. It is the enjoyer alone who always and everywhere abides as the object of enjoyment. Or, constantly attentive, and perceiving the entire universe as play, he who has this awareness (samvitti) is undoubtedly liberated in this very life.[46]

Ksemaraja – The Heart Of Recognition

Ksemaraja, a disciple of Abhinavagupta, and master in his own right, wrote in *The Heart Of Recognition:*

Whenever the extroverted conscious nature rests within itself, external objectivity is withdrawn and consciousness is established in the inner abode of peace which threads through the flux of awareness in every externally emanated state. Thus Turiya, the Goddess of Consciousness, is the union of creation, persistence and destruction. She emanates every individual cycle of creation and withdraws it. Eternally full of things and yet void of diversity She is both and yet neither, shining radiantly as non-successive consciousness alone.[47]

Geshe Rinpoche – The Black Tara

In the Hindu tradition sacred temple carvings often depict Gods and Goddesses in ecstatic union. The ancient Hindus, unfettered by modern notions of sex as a non-spiritual animal act of man, recognized ecstasy as a manifestation of the union of God and mankind. China Galland, in her autobiographical search for the feminine God within, *Longing for Darkness,* encountered in

Switzerland, a Gelupka Tibetan Geshe, Champa Lodra Rinpoche. Geshe Rinpoche relates the story of the female deity, the Black Tara:

> *Many countless aeons ago, in another kalpa [time] altogether, in the time of the Buddha Ngadra, there lived a princess named Yeshe Dawa, Wisdom Moon. She made innumerable offerings to Buddha Ngadra and the spiritual assembly, as the result of which she grew very close to becoming enlightened herself.*
>
> *"If you pray for a man's form, you will become enlightened in this very lifetime," the monks told her.*
>
> *"Man, woman, the self, the person—all these phenomena have no true existence," said Yeshe Dawa. "They only exist as projections of our incorrect conception of the world."*
>
> *"In actuality, they do not exist in and of themselves. They have no separate, independent existence, so there is no need for me to change myself into a man. Ideas of "male" and "female" always delude worldly people. Many wish to gain enlightenment in a man's form, but few wish to work for the benefit of sentient beings in a female form."*
>
> *"Therefore I will remain in a woman's form until reaching enlightenment and thus I will turn the wheel of Dharma, working for the benefit of all living beings, until the world of samsara is empty and all suffering ended."*
>
> *"You," Yeshe Dawa, the Buddha Ngadra prophesied, "will reach enlightenment in the form of Buddha Tara." Just as he foretold, she became fully enlightened and worked to free all living beings from sufferings in the world.*[48]

Lilian Silburn – Lalla, Kashmiri Poetess

Lilian Silburn in her excellent exploration of tantric sexuality and the awakening of enlightenment, *Kundalini: The Energy Of The Depths,* quotes Lalla, a mystic poetess of ancient Kashmir:[49]

> *With a rein did I hold back my thought.*
> *By ardent practice did I bring together the vital airs of my ten nadis.*[50]
> *Therefore did the digit of the moon melt and descend unto me.*
> *And a void become merged within the Void.*[51]

Lalla suggestively subdues the vital breath, rhythmically praising the potency of the pranava OM:

> *I locked the doors and windows of my body.*
> *I seized the thief of my vital airs,*
> *And controlled my vital breath.*
> *I bound him tightly in the closet of my heart,*

And with the whip of the pranava did I flay him.
When by concentration of my thoughts
I brought the pranava under my control,
I made my body like a blazing coal.
The six paths I traversed and gained the seventh,
And then did I, Lalla, reach the place of illumination.[52]

Mark Dyczkowski discusses the creative of the light of consciousness and the power of Siva:[53]

Perceptions could not take place were consciousness to be constantly at rest with itself. Completely immersed in its own indeterminate nature, nothing could be manifest at all. On the other hand, if consciousness were to be entirely emergent as the manifest universe, it could never be consciously experienced. The apparent ontological distinction between absolute and the relative, the infinite and the finite, is thus reducible to an epistemic distinction between two different modes of knowledge. The cognitive power of consciousness is its capacity to shift back and forth between these two modes and, as it does so, select some of the countless potential forms merged within it to make them externally manifest.[54]
The light of consciousness, full to overflowing with innumerable phenomena, thus separates some of them from itself, while at the same time limiting its own nature to appear as the individual (mayiya) subject set apart from the object. Perception takes place when this limited subject is affected by the 'shade' (chaya) cast upon it by the object. As the pulse of awareness moves from the expanded, undivided state to the contracted, limited condition and back again at each instant, novel perceptions are generated and the world of experience is thus constantly renewed. Thus this energy, like those of will and action, is essentially Siva's creative power (svantrya) which is the vibration (spanda) of consciousness through which He generates all things.[55]

Don Juan explains to Carlos how the miracle of assembling the world in consciousness occurs:

"When we, as serious adult human beings, look at a tree," he said, "our assemblage points align an infinite number of emanations and achieve a miracle. Our assemblage points make us perceive a cluster of emanations that we call tree."
    He explained that the assemblage point not only effects the alignment needed for perception, but also obliterates the alignment of certain emanations in order to arrive at a greater refinement of perception, a skimming, a tricky human construct with no parallel.
    He said that the new seers had observed that only humans were capable of further clustering the clusters of emanations. He used the

Spanish word for skimming, desnate, to describe the act of collecting the most palatable cream off the top of a container of boiled milk after it cools. Likewise, in terms of perception, man's assemblage point takes some part of the emanations already selected for alignment and makes a more palatable construct with it.[56]

Don Juan warns Carlos that we forget that we have constructed the world we perceive through our commanding the assemblage point to align the world as it does. Once the warrior learns to *see*, he can move his assemblage point from within. Having gained the power to move the assemblage point, the warrior *sees* that the world is created by the fixation of the assemblage point on the luminous body of consciousness. The warrior who has lost the human form *sees* that nothing matters more than anything else. Never having been anywhere, the warrior has no place to return. He reassembles the world through the exercise of his controlled folly, and lives out his life with total awareness in total freedom:

"The new seers burn with the force of alignment," don Juan went on, "with the force of 'will', which they have turned into 'intent' through a life of impeccability. 'Intent' is the alignment of all the amber emana-tions of awareness, so it is correct to say that total freedom means total awareness."

"Freedom is the Eagle's gift to man. Unfortunately, very few men understand that all we need, in order to accept such a magnificent gift, is to have sufficient energy."[57]

4. THE NATURE OF CONSCIOUSNESS

Dependent Arising and Emptiness

In Buddhist terminology, formulated some twenty five hundred years ago, everything that can be thought of can be viewed as a dependent arising. Whatever we view, whether particle or gross object, is tied intrinsically to, and is an aspect of the system or person attempting to obtain objective information regarding the object under consideration.

This is important to understand because we are taught from the moment we begin to speak that words are meaningful representations of the things they point towards. When we say brown, or tree, or sweet, we ordinarily view the object we are considering as possessing the attributes we project. The Buddha and generations of meditators have experienced the union of emptiness and appearance. Sugar cannot be said to be sweet on its own side. It is only when ingested that sugar has the attribute of sweetness. Likewise, the rough texture of the bark of a tree is not experiencing roughness on its own side; it is only after we come into contact with the tree do we experience roughness. What sugar or tree is, prior to our experience of it, is ineffable or empty. The Buddha realized that all of our experience is codependent with the object or system under consideration. He further stated that appearance and emptiness are in union. This is not to be memorized or believed, but rather to be appropriated with certainty, by meditating upon the true nature of the mind.

Nagarjuna – Dependent Arising

Nagarjuna, often referred to as the second Buddha, in some very complex philosophical discussions that we will only lightly touch upon here, argued that the very nature of consciousness is a dependent arising. He argued that it must be that the nature of the viewer, or person viewing this dependent field must also be dependent. It cannot be that if all that I view cannot be accurately perceived, that I as the organizer of this field of experience can view myself with any greater certainty of verifiable characteristics:

We state that whatever is dependent arising, that is emptiness. That is dependent upon convention. That itself is the middle path.
A thing that is not dependently arisen is not evident. For that reason, a thing that is non-empty is indeed not evident.[58]

Nagarjuna made a very bold assertion about the nature of reality. In the first statement Nagarjuna tells us that whatever we view cannot be validated on its own side as having the attributes we ascribe to the object. When I view your face and assemble appearance where does the appearance reside? If I ask you to relate to me the appearance of your face, you will be unable to respond. I can differentiate your face from all the others that I know; however, the basis for this differentiation is arbitrary, and dependent. The appearance of your face cannot be represented to me by you, the possessor of the face. The appearance of your face, oddly enough appears to reside uniquely within my consciousness. Having no veridical nature on its own side means the face is empty of inherent essence.

In the second statement, the middle path is synonymous with appearance (dependent arising) and emptiness. Absolute existence or nonexistence regarding that which is dependently arisen and empty can neither be affirmed nor negated. In the manner of a Zen koan, such as the famous "sound of one hand clapping", when we come to a place in consciousness beyond the ability of words to express meaning, we drop the argument and reside in appearance and emptiness. While it is interesting to wrestle with Nagarjuna's or don Juan's concepts, they are finally only pointers to an ineffable reality beyond words or ultimate knowing.

The third statement takes the position that that which is not dependently arisen is not evident. There is no object without an observer, and that which is not observed is not evident. Only that which is in union with appearance and emptiness is evident. If it is non-empty it cannot be evident. All of this would be philosophical mind games if it were not quite apparent to an experienced meditator, from an experiential point of view, that Nagarjuna is not only making a linguistic connotation about the nature of reality, he is also making an observation in consciousness. The nature of our experience in consciousness, whether it is the taste of chocolate or the color blue, can only be pointed towards through language, and is ultimately an appearance in union with emptiness.

Gadjin Nagao – Ultimate Meaning

Gadjin M. Nagao, Professor Emeritus in the Department of Buddhist Studies at Kyoto University, elaborates upon the two truths of ultimate meaning and worldly convention. If the relationship between emptiness and dependent co-arising is the warp running tautly through the fabric of Madhyamika thought, the two truths of ultimate meaning and worldly convention comprise the woof. Professor Nagao describes three aspects of ultimate meaning:

> The first aspect of ultimate meaning is that of the object (arthaparamartha), which is suchness (tathata). Suchness has to be realized personally and immediately (saksat-kriya), inasmuch as it is the ultimately meaningful object that constitutes realized wisdom. Here the term ultimate (parama) meaning (artha) is interpreted as the object of ultimate understanding (paramasya jnanasyarthah), in other words, as the object and content of world-transcending wisdom.
>
> The second aspect of ultimate meaning is that of attainment (praptiparamartha), or cessation (nirvana), as fully purified suchness. Suchness is that to which one becomes enlightened, that which is realized and attained through the conversion of support (asraya-paravrtti-laksana). Here, the term ultimate (parama) meaning (artha) refers to the final end of meaning (arthasya paramah), where the term artha indicates "benefit", namely, the benefit of cessation liberated from all misfortune that is the final goal of all practice. It is described as the highest benefit because it pervades all conditioned and unconditioned states of being.
>
> The third aspect of ultimate meaning is that of attainment (pratipatti-paramartha), or the path (marga) that leads to ultimate (parama) meaning (artha) is interpreted as "the meaning of that which is ultimate" (paramo syarthah), referring to the path whose object is suchness and whose objective is cessation. By following such an ultimate and aiming at it as one's goal, the path becomes an aspect and manifestation of ultimate meaning, even though the path itself belongs to the realm of conditioned being.[59]

Worldly convention is dependently co-arising with ultimate meaning. The distinction to be understood here is that worldly convention is not to be negated. If you ask me how to get to New York, I can tell you. If you ask me what New York is, I cannot tell you. It is neither the buildings, the streets, the people nor the location; it is all of that and ultimately beyond any final description. On its own side there is a New York of worldly convention, but not a New York of ultimate meaning. The meditator experiences the relationship of worldly convention and ultimate meaning as the union of emptiness and dependent co-arising, neither having more weight than the other. He sees that consciousness is surrounded on all sides by a world of co-dependent arising, and that he as the assembler and organizer of all that he purveys, is not apart from appearance and emptiness. The nondual nature of consciousness is established through worldly convention, and transcended in ultimate meaning. The objective of cessation is not a freezing over of the mind, but rather the beginning of the establishment of the human spirit in truth through discerning wisdom, and faith through union with ultimate meaning.

Je Yanggonpa cuts through the entanglement of concepts:

Any appearance emerging through the five senses
Is the luster of an unceasing flux.
That which arises from the sense objects without any mental clinging
Is the nature of nonarising [emptiness].
Even when attachment to appearance has not ceased,
It is sublimated to natural meditation.
Perceiving emptiness through appearance without discrimination
Is the inner process of elevation.
Do not view appearances as being deficient,
But abandon your attachment to them.
You will penetrate the expanse of the meditation of one flavor.[60]

The mind's abiding nature is inseparably united with appearances. The meditator has erased the perception of interior and exterior realities, and abides in the nondual, one flavor of appearance and emptiness.

Don Juan – *Not-doing*

Don Juan teaches Carlos Castaneda about the practical aspects of the union of appearance and emptiness or *doing* and *not-doing*. Carlos has been staring fixedly for some time at a pebble placed upon a boulder. Carlos task is to join the two, in *not-doing*. Don Juan tells Carlos that it is his *doing* that keeps the pebble and the boulder separate. After attempting this exercise for some length of time without success, don Juan tells Carlos to bury the pebble and change the *doing* of leaving a small pebble lying around into an act of *not-doing* and power by burying the pebble. Carlos heavy concern has changed the pebble into 'something quite unappealing'. Carlos asks don Juan:

> "*Is all this true, don Juan?*"
>
> "*To say yes or no to your question is doing. But since you are learning not-doing I have to tell you that it really doesn't matter whether or not all this is true. It is here that a warrior has a point of advantage over the average man. An average man cares that things are either true or false, but a warrior doesn't. An average man proceeds in a specific way with things that he knows are true, and in a different way with things that he knows are not true. If things are said to be true, he acts and believes in what he does. A warrior, on the other hand, acts in both instances. If things are said to be true, he would act in order to do doing. If things are said to be untrue, he would still act in order to do not-doing. See what I mean?*" [61]

For don Juan, when a warrior is engaged in *not-doing* he is feeling the world, rather than engaging the world through the inner dialog. In this mode the warrior is aware of both *doing* and *not-doing*, and is immersed in neither. He is the fluid witness of the tonal and the nagual, or appearance and emptiness. It is Carlos heavy concern that has shifted his attention away from the center of his awareness, and into an internal discussion or *doing*. The power of *not-doing* would have revealed the union of pebble, boulder, and Carlos, in the one-flavor of appearance and emptiness or nondual consciousness. To be all tonal or all nagual is to be lost in either worldly convention or nihilistic emptiness. It is the art of the warrior and man of knowledge to reside at the third point, the union of worldly convention and ultimate meaning, fluidly balancing tonal and nagual.

Don Juan attempts to have Carlos Castaneda see that the objects of the world are constructed through our doing.

> "*Take that rock for instance. To look at it is doing, but to see it is not-doing. I had to confess that his words were not making sense to me.*"
>
> "*Oh yes they do!*" *he exclaimed.* "*But you are convinced that they don't because that is your doing. That is the way you act towards me and the world.*"

He again pointed to the rock.

"That rock is a rock because of all the things you know how to do to it,"
he said. "I call that doing. A man of knowledge, for instance, knows that
the rock is a rock only because of doing. So if he doesn't want the rock to
be a rock all he has to do is not-doing. See what I mean?" [62]

Don Juan informs Carlos Castaneda how *not-doing* revitalizes our
connection with the mysterious:

He reminded me that he had described to me in the past the concept of
stopping the world. He said that stopping the world was as necessary for
sorcerers as reading and writing was for me. It consisted of introducing
a dissonant element into the fabric of everyday behavior for the purposes
of halting the otherwise smooth flow of ordinary events—events which
were catalogued in our minds by our reason.

The dissonant element was called "not-doing" or the opposite of
"doing." "Doing" was anything that was part of a whole for which we
had a cognitive account. "Not-doing" was an element that did not belong
in the charted whole." [63]

To confuse the menu of words with the meal of direct knowing is
to rob life of the richness of silent experience. To be trapped in the
menu of society's words for the entirety of this one precious life is
tragic. It is possible to awaken to the richness of the mystery of
dependent arising and emptiness and take back one's life from the
abyss of society's collective insanity. To awaken from the dream and
experience the meal of life is to be fully alive. The means to awaken
is through the mastery of awareness.

5. THE NATURE OF THE SELF

Bhavanakrama – Manifestations Of Mind

It would seem from Nagarjuna's discussion that on my own side, and yours as well, you and I have no truly verifiable nature located either within ourselves or anywhere else for that matter! We seem to exist very much like the electron, having intrinsic aspects belonging neither solely to ourselves, nor to an independent observer.

The first Bhavanakrama elaborates on the nature of self.

> *Meditate upon the nonselfhood of all things, which are comprised of the five psychological aggregates, the twelve sense formations, and the eighteen realms of elements. Ultimately, apart from being manifestations of the mind, these aggregates, sense formations, and elements do not have an independent reality. No object of attachment can exist, as the essence of reality itself is non-existent. Their reduction to particles and finally to infinitesimal proportions will show this. Determining reality in this manner, one should contemplate that from phenomena, childish sentient beings have mistaken the mind's manifestations for external reality in much the same way as a dreamer holds his dreams to be true. Ultimately, all these are but manifestations of the mind.*[64]

When we view an inanimate structure we are not on safer ground in regard to absolute attributes. A room, for example, does not have absolute color, form or size without an observer. A mosquito or dog might perceive a much larger, monochrome cavern. We are not attempting to negate the conventional agreement that there is in some sense a room. What we are attempting to establish is the dependently arisen nature of the room. The room does not have the qualities you or I attribute to it when no one is present. It is not 'brown' or 'romantic' or 'Spartan' or 'luxurious' or anything for that matter without a person present who imputes some aspect in consciousness upon the room or its contents. We can agree that we live in a world of familiar objects in the conventional sense. In the ultimate sense the world of objects are dependently arising within our consciousness. And this dependent arising in the transcendental sense has some very important implications, as we shall see.

Nagarjuna – Valid Relative Phenomena

The School of Valid Relative Phenomena examines the relativistic view of phenomena:

> *Nagarjuna and his spiritual son Aryadeva described the way the School of Valid Relative Phenomena [Svatantrika-Madhyamaka] determined the vision of reality. It holds that nothing essential or real can be found in all the dualistic realities when they are thoroughly investigated through logical analysis, known as the nonexistence of one and many [absolute entities]. It accepts an experiential phenomenon described as nonconceptual awareness, which is well-settled in its supraperceptive simplicity. Hence this transcending state is designated as inmost discerning wisdom.[65]*

Nagarjuna and Aryadeva having examined appearances state that the nature of apprehended objects cannot be ascertained exclusive of the observer. Thus, an observer, surrounded by ultimately unknowable objects, is himself without absolute attribute. When the observer attempts to define his own size, shape, color or nature, he is forced to use the objects found in apparent dualistic realities as reference indices. Since these objects have been found by prior analysis to be non-veridical on their own side, the observer is likewise settled in supraperceptive simplicity, the union of appearance and emptiness. Realizing this state is known as discerning wisdom:

> *Prasangika-Madhyamika holds as the essential vision a transcending awareness of the unity of perceptive appearances and their inherent void, rejecting the two extreme modes—absolute reality and nihility. Meditators should seek to realize this perfect view of reality.[66]*

Savari illuminates the perfect view of reality that is without self-nature, detached from duality, and free from striving and seeking:

> *For a realized mind the duality*
> *Of meditation and meditator do not exist.*
> *Just as space cannot perceive itself as an object,*
> *So emptiness cannot meditate on itself.*
> *In a state of nondual awareness*
> *The diverse perceptions blend uninterruptedly,*
> *Like milk and water, into one flavor of great bliss.[67]*

Don Juan – The Mirror Of Self-Reflection

Don Juan utilizes *not-doing* as a means to break the mirror of self-reflection. *Not-doing* because it is outside the normal inventory of man's inner dialogue collapses the continuity of the world constructed in consciousness. Don Juan tells Carlos of the difficulty of explaining *not-doing*:

> *"I am going to tell you something very simple but very difficult to perform; I am going to talk to you about not-doing, in spite of the fact that there is no way to talk about it, because it is the body that does it."* [68]

Don Juan's *not-doing* can only be effectively spoken of after one has *stopped the world*. When we are in the clutches of the tonal and have become so solid that the internal dialogue rules our being we are in the midst of *doing* the world. We see our problems as insurmountable and may believe that they will never diminish. We feel trapped by the perceived circumstance as interpreted by our inner dialogue. Our total attention is transfixed by our belief system. We are totally immersed in a trance-like projection in consciousness of fear. The world has suddenly become overwhelmingly real through our doing. We are convinced that really this time we have had it! I call this a crisis in faith. We forget that we have arrived at this dimensionless moment in life by some mysterious grace of Being. We have in the past surmounted whatever obstacles that have come our way—or we would no longer Be! The lessons we have learned have been learned because we grew in our ability to assimilate new knowledge as a consequence of mastering new difficulty. Without difficulty life is without challenge. Helen Keller was born without sight or hearing. Through great struggle she acquired penetrating wisdom, and observed *that life is either a great challenge or nothing at all.* When our inner dialogue stops with assuredness we relinquish our projection. When we use the doings of the tonal for the purpose of projecting the future we eventually fall victim to our own doings. We have never, with any certainty, been able to look into our crystal ball and penetrate this mysterious moment. Nevertheless, we repeatedly take our inventory of self-created projections and nonsensically suffer at our own hands, or more accurately, suffer as a consequence of our nonexistent fortune telling ability.

Not-doing is the surrender of the tonal, in total faith, to the mystery of the feeling of being, the nagual:

"The most durable lines that a man of knowledge produces come from the middle of the body," he said, "But he can also make them with his eyes."
"Are they real lines?"
"Surely."
"Can you see them and touch them?"
"Let's say that you can feel them. The most difficult part about the warrior's way is to realize that the world is a feeling. When one is not-doing, one is feeling the world, and one feels the world through its lines." [69]

Don Juan has the apprentice directly experience that both *doing* and *not-doing* point towards the ineffable. Once the disciple has succeeded in balancing the tonal and the nagual, reason and will, he has sufficient power to stop the world at will, and arrive at the third point, silent knowledge:

The old nagual [Elias] explained that the position of silent knowledge was called the third point because in order to get to it one had to pass the second point, the place of no pity.

He said that don Juan's assemblage point had acquired sufficient fluidity for him to be double, which had allowed him to be in both the place of reason and in the place of silent knowledge, either alternately or at the same time.[70]

At the root of Carlos difficulty, and ours as well, is the clinging to reality induced through words. *The place of reason* is the conventional world, spun through the world of the inner dialog and social consensus. *The place of silent knowledge* is the union of appearance and emptiness or ultimate meaning. Becoming aware of both aspects of our mysterious being, *the double*, frees our assemblage point to be simultaneously aware of both aspects of awareness, *the place of reason* and *the place of silent knowledge*. When we continually renew our world through the inner dialog or reason, we become trapped in our own words and concepts. We forget that we are the author of our entrapment, and cannot break the self-imposed cycle of doubt, anxiety or despair. While we struggle as prisoners of words, and the tyrannical self, we fear the void between thoughts. To search within, and find absolutely nothing, is to confront the awesome possibility of our egoic, if not actual death, and self-transcendence.

We are never truly functionally attached to the objects, conceptions and perceptions in consciousness. The egoic self arises as a feeling of separation or difference in consciousness. When we falsely perceive separation or difference between consciousness and the objects, conceptions and perceptions in consciousness, we recoil into dualism. We believe we are really looking out at reality, rather than being that in which apparent reality arises. The illusory separation in consciousness, of consciousness into apparent subject and object, is the root cause of suffering.

Being *the double* dissolves the apparent or illusory subject and object in consciousness as the nondual union of appearance and emptiness. When we are able to see the self from the vantage point of *the double* we are simultaneously aware of the place of reason and the place of silent knowledge, the union of appearance and emptiness. When the illusory nature of the self is revealed with absolute certainty—its death is imminent. However, our egoic death is not the absolute termination of our being, but rather the seed of our metamorphosis into transcendental being.

When we *see* that we know absolutely nothing with certainty— when we *see* that words cannot penetrate the mystery of this magical moment—we are free of the tyranny of conceptualizing mind. Experiencing the double is freedom of awareness, and the beginning of our journey beyond the veil of knowledge. We *see* that we have never experienced a place of no thing, nor one of absolute thing, only the boundary in between. The nature of our mystery as luminous beings is related in the *Bhagavad-Gita* to Arjuna, the seeker of knowledge. Krishna, the mystic seer, assures Arjuna:

> *Nothing of non-being comes to be,*
> *nor does being cease to exist;*
> *the boundary between these two*
> *is seen by men who see reality.*[71]

The Sutralamkara illuminates nondual reality:

> *Understand that nothing exists apart from the mind.*
> *Know that the mind itself is unreal*
> *An intelligent person, comprehending the unreality of the two,*
> *Settles in the expanse of the nondual reality.*[72]

Donald Williams – Disintegration Of Awareness

We live in, and as a mysterious plane of being which we continually trivialize and make ordinary through *doing*. The *not-doing* of worldly convention is nondual being—transcendental, mysterious, and numinous. To live without fear in the magnificent unknown, we must learn how to harmonize worldly convention *(doing)* and ultimate meaning *(not-doing)*. Donald Williams, in his profoundly insightful psychological investigation, *Border Crossings*, discusses the disintegration of the conventional self of Carlos Castaneda:

> *Carlos experience of the disintegration of his awareness into separate particles, and the subsequent reunion of those particles, tells us something further about the nature of consciousness. Our consciousness is made up of a plurality of souls, of independently functioning units of consciousness. We can easily recognize this fact in terms of our thinking, feeling, sensation, intuition, instinctive responses, and so on, but Carlos carries this plurality further. Let us imagine that in one moment we are observing something with our eyes while at the same time following a train of thought, while at the same time experiencing some sensation in our knees, and so on in a continually changing arrangement of consciousness from moment to moment. In the account of Carlos' leap we see all these separate awarenesses going separate ways. These nuggets are held together, however, by the guardian spirit on the side of the tonal[73] and by will on the side of the nagual.[74] Carlos has learned to trust this instinctive cohesiveness of his individuality. Most people legitimately fear that a profound experience of the unconscious could lead to disintegration, and thus the guardian is encouraged to become a vigilant guard. The warrior, however, organizes his life and tunes his will to such a degree that he can experience himself as the one and the many.[75]*

Ordinarily we do not see birth and death as opposite and joined sides of the coin, intrinsically and mysteriously bound. We believe that we know about death, when in fact we know of few who can tell us about it or even verify it's existence. The termination of physical life is assumed to be the end of our existence. A caterpillar spinning its cocoon might make a similar assumption regarding the eminent termination of its existence, but how accurate would that assumption be? We identify ourselves with our bodies and are convinced that the destruction of the physical self coincides with total annihilation. Through meditation we acquire knowledge of *the double*, and through nondual awareness learn to balance the *doing* of the tonal, the self-created world of words, with the mystery of the nagual, the place of silent knowledge. Savari clarifies that which is indefinable, beyond imagination, transcends birth and death, and is the absolute subject of subjectivity:

> *In the process of searching for all that manifests as mind and matter*
> *There is neither anything to be found nor is there any seeker,*
> *For to be unreal is to be unborn and unceasing*
> *In the three periods of time.*
> *That which is immutable*
> *Is the state of great bliss.*[76]

Mahamudra – Nondual Awareness

The meditator delves still further into the analysis of consciousness, and experiences the ultimate unification of appearance and its intrinsic emptiness in nondual awareness. Having arrived at the inescapable juncture of egoic disintegration, the meditator can either disassemble into madness or integrate his newfound wisdom. The stabilization of this new experience is arrived at through the study of consciousness, ultimately unifying tranquility and wisdom in effortless mastery. Mahasiddha Kotali explains:

> *When ordinary mind awakens its inmost recess*
> *And the six sensory perceptions are purified,*
> *A stream of bliss will flow incessantly.*
> *All designations are meaningless and become the source of misery.*
> *Settle the mind in its primal simplicity and nonmeditative state.*[77]

Je Gampopa describes ordinary mind:

> *If at this moment one wishes to achieve liberation from the cycle of existence, one must recognize ordinary mind, for it is the root of all things. That which is designated as "ordinary mind" is one's own awareness. Left in its natural state, this awareness remains unstained by any [nonordinary] perceptive forms, unmuddled by any levels of existential consciousness, and unclouded by dullness, depression or thought. If one has discovered the identity of that mind one has discovered self-cognizing awareness. If one fails to gain such an understanding, this ordinary mind remains with the coemergence of ignorance. However, the understanding of that mind is called*

awareness, the essence, the coemergent self-knowing, ordinary mind, unmodulated simplicity, nondiscrimination, and luminous clarity.[78]

The importance lies in the experience of the essence of mind, not solely in the understanding of the above words. The space-like intrinsic nature of ordinary mind must be experienced through the mastery of tranquil absorption, and penetrating analysis. The third *Bhavanakrama* describes how to maintain bare or nondiscriminatory awareness:

> *Thus, one should understand that perfect analysis precedes the contemplative state of "no memory" and "no mental activity", revealed in the holy teaching, for perfect analysis alone can effectively bring about this nondiscriminatory state of "no memory" and "no mental construction." Thus, when a yogin investigates through his discerning intellect, he does not consciously cognize the absolute emergence of reality at that moment, in the past, or in the future. At that moment he enters the meditative state described as "no memory" or "no mental activity." Only by reaching this state will he realize the emptiness of reality and will then eliminate all intertwined misconceptions.*[79]

Identifying the contemplative state with intrinsic awareness, in accordance with Dzogpa Chenpo, Jigmed Lingpa explains:

> *In Dzogpa Chenpo, by contemplating and remaining without modification, in the state of the continuum of primordial wisdom, which is free from elaborations, spontaneously arisen, transcending the mind, free from actions and pacification of mind and mental events, the sudden defilements of the manifestation power (of the Intrinsic Awareness) disappear naturally.*[80]

6. TRANSCENDING THE DUST OF KNOWLEDGE

Seeking Illumination

Carlos Castaneda is an author whose work should not go unread by anyone on the path of self-development. During the nineteen sixties, Castaneda, a young doctoral candidate (later professor of Anthropology at the University of California), began, through his extraordinary writings, to make a great and mystical impact among college students across the nation. Castaneda also captured the imagination of academia, as well as millions of international readers of all ages and persuasions during the next thirty years. An entire generation began to explore, through Castaneda's *The Teachings of don Juan,* and a series of subsequent books, the possibility of a reality not fixed in time and space, but transcending the very notion of time and space. For those of you who have not encountered the Central American sorcerer and seer, don Juan, it is interesting to note that during their first meeting, Castaneda had attempted to solicit the old Yaqui Indian, don Juan, to teach him about the use of medicinal plants, especially the hallucinogen peyote. Eventually Castaneda learned more than he ever wanted to know about peyote, and more than he thought possible about himself.

At first Castaneda saw don Juan as just an "eccentric", old Mexican Indian; of medium height, short white hair, dark skin, deep wrinkles, and a penetrating gaze—with eyes that seemed to shine with a light of their own.[81] Having no basis upon which to assess the extraordinary, how many of us could recognize a Buddha, Christ, or don Juan, if we had, as Castaneda had, literally stumbled into a masters presence? Castaneda had, in fact, encountered a master seer, a man of knowledge. Fortunately for millions of readers around the world, Castaneda, with consummate skill, began documenting his meetings with his teacher, the Central American sorcerer, don Juan. Some time later in their relationship Carlos asked don Juan about the advisability of making public esoteric teachings, such as *the sorcerer's explanation,* and don Juan, most sagely, responded:

> *"Personal power decides who can or who cannot profit by a revelation; my experiences with my fellow man have proven to me that very, very*

few of them would be willing to listen; and of those few who listen even fewer would be willing to act on what they have listened to; and of those who are willing to act even fewer have enough personal power to profit by their acts. So, the matter about secrecy about the sorcerers' explanation boils down to routine as empty as any other routine." [82]

Don Juan – The Assemblage Point

For don Juan the key to sorcery is moving the assemblage point, a shift in the level of awareness. Don Juan revealed that we all experience this shift, sometimes through fright or illness, deprivation or stress. Although we find ourselves experiencing extraordinary states of awareness, having no familiarity with these states we forget and revert quickly back to habitual modes of perception. Don Juan discusses the assemblage point:

"When a movement of the assemblage point is maximized", he went on, "both the average man or the apprentice in sorcery becomes a sorcerer, because by maximizing that movement, continuity is shattered beyond repair."

"How do you maximize that movement?" I asked.

"By curtailing self-reflection," he replied. "Moving the assemblage point or breaking one's continuity is not the real difficulty. The real difficulty is having energy. If one has energy, once the assemblage point moves, inconceivable things are there for the asking."

Don Juan explained that man's predicament is that he intuits his hidden resources, but he does not dare use them. This is why sorcerers say that man's plight is the counterpoint between his stupidity and his ignorance. He said that man needs now, more than ever, to be taught new ideas that have to do exclusively with his inner world—sorcerers' ideas, not social ideas, ideas pertaining to man facing the unknown, facing his personal death. Now, more than anything else, he needs to be taught the secrets of the assemblage point. [83]

The sorcerer's ideas are powerful facilitators of wisdom. This is a wisdom that destroys inner psychological delusion, and is the seed of transcending awareness and personal fulfillment. The sorcerer's wisdom ultimately reveals the supreme vision of man's purpose in the cosmos. In the Mahamudra tradition, Tsongkhapa, an ancient sorcerer, reveals the illuminating nature of wisdom:

Wisdom is the eye that looks at the profound nature of reality;
It is the means to cut the root of samsara.

An inexhaustible source of qualities praised in the scriptures,
It is renowned as the brilliant light that illuminates the darkness of
delusion.[84]

It is ironic that most of us look for illumination outside of our own experience, when the ultimate illumination comes from within. How many of us would seek out a guru to tell us of the taste of chocolate or to relate to us the experience of love? And yet most of us expect to be illumined by some spiritual authority. Often, nowhere in our experience or that of anyone we know, has such an illumination been forthcoming. In our search for salvation we most often give obeisance to the leaders of the sect in which we are born — although we know of no one who has truly been saved, nor do we have the vaguest notion of what being saved means. We often go to our religious authorities with only surface questions, perhaps because we are afraid to examine too deeply. For the most part, our religious institutions encourage doctrine, and discourage discerning wisdom; and we in turn pray that obedience will yield God's grace. Often, we are too close to the myths of our own religion and culture to dispassionately examine them.

Transcending the Dust Of Time

An example of a myth, widespread throughout the world, is the myth of "time" as being something substantially real. This myth is created by nearly universal consensus, and by the psycho-linguistic construction of units of time. We have just about absolute belief in the duration of the second, minute, day of the week, month, etc. When I tell you we have been conversing for one hour, you believe that you know precisely what that means. For most of us time is as real as the reading on our watches. Consider, though, the relative nature of time. While you are waiting in line to pay a highway toll, an hour might seem like a day. While you are engaged in your favorite activity, an hour might seem like ten minutes. If the experience of an hour or any other unit of time can vary, are units of time valid in some inherent way that we have not yet examined or revealed? Closer examination only reveals that time appears elastic in experience, and empty of inherent duration on its own side. Final examination reveals time as having no side of its own — outside of consciousness! Viewing time in this manner, we are again facing the nagual. Of course, in the conventional sense time exists; but that is a story with which we or our tonal, are all too familiar.

Has it ever occurred to you how much thought is given to past and future occurrences, and how little control we have over either. In each and every moment of time our apparent circumstance changes, but we as the observer of the passing scene remain the same. We label a remembered moment as the past, and those moments yet to come as the future. Remembered moments, while they often give us very good representations of what has occurred do not actually bring the *past* into the present. In a sense, in order to consider a *past* occurrence we must conjure an illusion or mental image in consciousness. This mental image in mind represents the *past*. When we confuse the symbol, in this case the mental image, for the thing itself, we forget that the thing itself and its representation are not the same. For instance, the vocalization of the word *salt* is a sound wave which when converted in consciousness produces the representation of the substance, which in our language we commonly agree to be salt. The substance and the word representation are not the same. The vocalization of the word *past* is a sound wave which, when converted in consciousness, produces the representation of the event we commonly agree to represent as an occurrence that is not present. There is, however, a substantial difference, more than words can bridge, between representation and the actual object of representation. The substance called salt can be brought into present experience to be directly appropriated by our senses. The event we call past cannot be brought into direct and present experience. The past cannot be brought into present experience because, even as events appear to occur in the present, they never are truly existent. Thus, a present time that is not truly existent is not a consequence of a nonexistent past, nor is it a foundation for a nonexistent future. Each apparent moment is devoid of the three periods of time. Take any present moment of experience, and it is intrinsically and solely tied to you—the witness in consciousness. Since no one else can witness exactly from the precise location in time-space, your representation and appropriation in consciousness of the present moment is unique to you. You are not merely witnessing the world at large, you are the world at large.

If you are in deep sleep, nothing arises in your world. When you awaken the world continues from your unique vantage point. However, your unique vantage point never becomes a universal experience such as *salt*. Just as the dream state experience never arises to become a verifiable reality, neither does your waking experience. In the conventional sense you and I can agree we are conversing together, but the personal appropriation of that event called conversation is without substance. The events of conversation and dreaming disappear into the vastness as quickly as they appear. In each and every moment of apparent now the events in consciousness appear only to disappear.

The National Bureau of Standards utilizes the constant rate of decaying radiation as a time standard. Ironically, nowhere in the universe is there an analog of a second, minute, hour or any other unit of time. Man has invented these units. There is no minute or other unit of time in nature. Time does not exist without space, and space is beyond dimension. The past, for instance, while you can consider it in memory, can never be recalled so thoroughly that it becomes a present reality. Do not confuse what is called memory for the thing itself—that construct in consciousness that occurs in the present moment that we label as past. Memory is not the same as past! Memory is a representation that occurs in the *now*! Past is not at all like a house key on your key chain, that you can pull out of your pocket or purse, and feel and see it grasped within your fingers. None of us have ever truly experienced the past, only the eternal now. And yet, our consciousness is always exploring, as if the past and the future were realities that could be shaped and controlled within the present.

Our delusion in consciousness makes it seem that the past and future are more pliable, more existent, than the eternally present now. The future is a shadow, just over the next hill. It never gets here. When the future appears to get here, it is already the present. Our mind wanders on and on, searching for some future state of being or security that never comes. We persist in this habit, willing to die to perpetuate it, rather than give up the tyranny of habits, desires and dream-like labyrinths of consciousness that dominate our lives. We almost continually contemplate future states of release, giving up this present moment for a future that never arrives. What appears in the now is constant anticipation and reflection. We often live devoid of present pleasures, either reviewing the past or in wait of the morrow. Look around you right now. Has tomorrow arrived? If it has, then what has happened to today? Or is the time, as always, just *now*?

We eat by the clock. We wear a wristwatch so that we are never truly removed from time and its obligations. We make love by the clock, hopefully losing ourselves in an all too brief ecstatic release of time, and space, and self. We experience the bliss of annihilation in orgasm, then the resumption of conventional time, and relinquish our mystical experience to trivial and discursive mind chatter. We may wish the pleasure could have lasted just a little longer, and without further reflection resume our captivity, and apparent safety, in ordinary modes of knowing. What draws us back again and again to this little death of self, with its accompaniment of intense, but brief pleasure? It is just one aspect of the spiritual urge to transcendence of the ego, a universal calling to the path of awareness, leading to enlightenment.

Often we confuse sexual activity with love, and rush towards sex as the means to relieve a temporary itch on the way to getting back to the real business of life. We wonder if we'll ever find true love, and the unique someone who will be the person of our dreams, while people who already love us are negated. Our internal chatter defines and limits who we are, and how we order our field of experience. It never occurs to us that there is infinitely more to love, sex, orgasm, spirit, and time, than that which is defined by verbalization. We wait for pauses in a conversation so that we can put forward our ideas, after having been only partially present to hear the other person's point of view. When the conversation lapses we rush in to fill the silence, as if chatter is more valuable than the purity of silence. And the longer the silence lasts, the more uncomfortable we become. We don't know how to be in silence with each other, or ourselves, and often rush anxiously to fill the lapses in conversation, or habitually occupy our time so that we do not have to be alone with ourselves.

Unfortunately, most of us never see that our ability to love, and our connection to the spirit, is seriously hampered by our obsession with material possession, success, and being lost in the labyrinth-like verbalizations of mind. Our lack of faith in the underlying ground of being is represented by our continual search for control. Without faith, each and every moment has at its root—anxiety. Our wealth, health, possessions, and self-esteem are continually monitored in order to prevent present or future loss. During the Great Depression men jumped from the roofs of tall buildings rather than continue life without the emblems and trappings of material success. When faced with similar loss, women simply moved to less costly living quarters. What other animal, besides man, defines self through possession? Is "success" merely to reach the end of life having the largest pile of rubbish? Through our incessant internal chatter we continuously project and refresh our view of apparent reality. When we begin to awaken from the stream of our internal dialogue we begin to see that what we had often expected to happen did not happen. We may find that the lessons we require to grow are gained through temporary setback. We may even learn that no acquisition brings lasting happiness, and that happiness is a state of being. Happiness is not a condition that can be lost or acquired through material possession. Our projections about what will happen, what has happened, and what is happening now, are so colored by our internal dialogue that it is often impossible to live genuinely, and free in the moment. Adi Da sings the definitive revelation of Happiness:

> *Happiness is Not An Object. If It were, What Native or Inherent Quality Would It Modify or limit?*
> *Happiness Is Inherently and Perfectly Subjective. And It Is Inherent To the Inherently Perfect Subject, or Consciousness Itself. Therefore, Happiness Is That Native or Original Quality (or Inherent Force Of Being) That Is Apparently Modified, Apparently Revealed, or Apparently Decreased By The Apparent Association Between Consciousness and Both Great Objects and lesser objects.*
> *To Seek Happiness As If It Were An Object (or To Identify With any conditionally Manifested objects or others, or Even To Allow It To Depend Upon any conditionally manifested objects or others) Is Absurd, An Always Already Benighted and UnHappy Quest, founded On A Fundamental Misunderstanding Of Happiness, (or Reality) Itself.*
> *To Seek Happiness (Rather Than To Realize It Inherently) Is To Be*

Possessed By the self-Contraction and To Be Motivated By it. Because Of the self-Contraction, What Is Inherent Ceases To Be Obvious, and, As A Result, the ego-"I" Seeks Among objects and others (and Even In the body-mind itself) For What Can Only Be found or Realized Inherently, In Place, In The Well Of Transcendental (and Inherently Spiritual, or Love-Blissful) Divine Being. Indeed, the ego-"I" Is Always Stressfully At Effort, In The Absurd Quest For Happiness and Consciousness.[85]

At birth we are without concept, prejudice, or belief. We adopt the language of our ancestors, incorporating without question the myth and taboo of our ancient, and often unillumined forefathers, and then wonder for the rest of our lives why we are suffering. We sanctify the edicts of our parents and teachers through total egoic assimilation of cultural and family platitudes. We are often willing to die, or at the very least, remain perpetually embarrassed and stifled, protecting ideas that were never truly our own. We wonder if there is a way out, but knowing no one who has escaped the tyranny of mind alive, we give it up as a lost cause. There are those, however, who have escaped alive, the yogi, or adept for example. The ancient Sanskrit word, *jivanmukti*, means the man who lives in freedom while alive. This can be you, if you are willing to explore the possibility. Growth is possible if the strangeness of new words and concepts does not cause you to recoil in fear of the unfamiliar, and the unknown. We must set aside time to discover, become familiar with, and deepen our spiritual awareness. Just as a violinist, or other artist seeks mastery through practice, so must we. Beyond the tyranny of the inner dialogue lies a mystery awaiting its master.

7. EXPLORING DREAMTIME

The Dream Body

I was walking down a red-carpeted office aisle. On either side of the aisle male and female workers were sitting at their desks engaged in a variety of office activity. I arrived at the mailroom, entered, and walked towards the letterboxes. Just then Charlie, a very tall former basketball player entered the mailroom and stood next to me. I looked up at Charlie, and said quite naturally, "Charlie, I'm in my dream body." He looked back somewhat incredulously. Perhaps, he didn't believe me, or was not familiar with the dream body. "Let me show you," I said, and bodily drifted up to the ceiling, floating high above Charlie's head. I was aware of myself as a bodily presence, not at all limited by reason, or gravity. Mouth gaping, Charlie finally sputtered, "I'm getting out of here."

At that moment the dream ended. I had known from the first moment I had spoken with Charlie that I was fast asleep in my bed at home, and simultaneously awake in the dream.

From a conventional point of view it could be said that my dream is less real than my time awake. I would ask you, however, how real is our time awake? Are you sure that as you sit there book in hand, your experience at this moment is more real than my dream? When you are asleep and dreaming, who is speaking for the characters in your dream? Is it not so, that ultimately you are the master puppeteer, the voice of all your dream characters? Where are the time and space boundaries of your dream? When you are having a meeting with friends, where does the meeting take place, at the meeting place, or in your consciousness? Where are the time and space boundaries of your present moment? What happened to a moment ago?

Don Juan – Dreaming

Don Juan discussed the nature of reality and dreaming with Carlos Castaneda in Journey to Ixtlan.

> "*Dreaming is real for a warrior because in it he can act deliberately, he can choose and reject, he can select from a variety of items those which*

lead to power, and then he can manipulate them, while in an ordinary dream he cannot act deliberately."
"Do you mean then, don Juan, that dreaming is real?"
"Of course it is real."
"As real as what we are doing now?"
  *"If you want to compare things, I can say that it is perhaps more real. In dreaming you have power; you can change things; you may find out countless concealed facts; you can control whatever you want." *[86]

Donald Williams, author of the excellent and perceptive, Border Crossings, A Psychological Perspective on Carlos Castaneda's Path of Knowledge, illuminates the double, and dreaming:

The double, don Juan says, is developed through dreaming; or more correctly, one becomes aware of the double in the process of dreaming. The double is the awareness of our luminosity, according to don Juan. We can interpret his statements to mean that through dream analysis, dreaming, active imagination and other forms of work on the unconscious, we become aware of the larger personality that exists in us. This larger personality is oneself, and yet it is more than we are capable of realizing in the realm of the tonal regardless of how much the ego self and the double begin to approximate each other. As the awareness of our luminosity, the double is the awareness of our totality that is both personal and suprapersonal, sacred and profane. The double is the "I" that witnesses and experiences the vaster realms of vision. The subtle body of active imagination does not experience the same limitations of time and space imposed upon us in waking life.[87]

Don Juan – Death And The Ticket To Freedom

The awareness of the double also heralds the beginning of the death of our personal self, and the coming into being of the transcendental self. The apprentice faces the actual death of the personal, or egoic self:

"My benefactor told me that a sorcerer's ticket to freedom was his death," don Juan went on. *"He said that he himself had paid with his life for that ticket to freedom, as had everyone else in his household. And that now we were equals in our condition of being dead."*
  "Am I dead too, don Juan?" I asked.
  "You are dead," he said. *"The sorcerer's grand trick, however, is to be aware that they are dead. Their ticket to impeccability must be wrapped in awareness. In that wrapping, sorcerers say, their ticket is kept in mint*

condition."
"For sixty years, I've kept mine in mint condition." [88]

Adi Da – Death Of The Self

Adi Da advises us to start the day without the encumbrance of the self:

> *But before you get involved with anything on any day, get up from bed and drop dead! First* <u>spiritually</u> *give yourself up to death before you get involved in anything you are likely to be attached to that day. Give yourself up to perfect surrender to God. Such surrender will involve loss of bodily consciousness and whatever else happens when you give yourself up, and then begin your associations. Give yourself up to God first by sacred acts in the company of others, such as prayers and chanting, and gradually begin your associations of the day. Then throughout the day maintain sacred occasions such as study and your personal and constant surrender to God directly, in the form of your actions.* [89]

Adi Da clarifies the "death" of the body-mind in Enlightenment:

> *".... when the body-mind is completely Absorbed, or Outshined, there is no remaining sense of "above" or "below", or "within", or "without", or "other". There is only Bliss the Transcendental Heart or Self. But this Condition of Absorption gives way again to the natural Condition of Whole Body Enlightenment. (If it did not, the body-mind would pass away in Divine Ecstasy.)"*

> *"Thus, the death of the Perfect Devotee is simply a matter of his permanent persistence in Divine Absorption, wherein the body-mind is Outshined and the conditional self dissolves forever in the Self of God."* [90]

Don Juan – Facing A New Direction

In *The Second Ring of Power*, the issue of the warrior's struggle to achieve the death of the self is addressed. Doña Soledad engages Carlos Castaneda in a veritable life and death battle. The Nagual don Juan, prior to Carlos' visit to doña Soledad, had given her elaborate instructions in order to effect the appropriation of Carlos' power. The preparation for this battle is long and arduous, and eventually results in the total transformation of Soledad. In order to accomplish this feat Soledad constructs a new room in her home with a baked clay mandala[91] floor. The construction of the mandala assists Soledad in facing a new direction. The transformation from dependent personality into self-actualized womanhood parallels the acquisition of self-confidence, and is commensurate with Soledad learning new skills. In *The Eagle's Gift* a corollary to Soledad's transformation occurs as Carlos is instructed in the art of stalking by Florinda Donner, one of the members of don Juan's group of warriors. Florinda explains that she is helping Carlos to turn his head:

> *When don Juan had described the concept of turning a warrior's head to face a new direction, I had understood it as a metaphor that depicted a change in attitude. Florinda said that that description was true, but it was no metaphor. It was true that stalkers turn their heads; however, they do not turn them to face a new direction, but to face time in a different way. Stalkers face the oncoming time. Normally we face time as it recedes from us. Only stalkers can change that and face time as it advances on them.[92]*

Having stopped the world, the meditator, or disciple is now capable of facing oncoming time. The facing of time as it advances upon the meditator does not mean that the meditator has merely changed his attention from viewing time as it recedes, to viewing time as it advances. The union of time-space and emptiness reveals the illusory nature of time, and the transformation-rebirth as sorcerer. The newly emergent sorcerer stands immutable at the center of space, or consciousness, the third point of reference, in ultimate simplicity, bliss and clarity.

Donald Williams – The Mandala

Donald Williams connects the symbolism of the mandala to the restructuring of Soledad's personality:

> *The design of the floor is obviously symbolic. It is a mandala, and as a mandala it has an integrating and centering effect. Because the lines are symmetric and converge at a center, the floor is a symbolic statement of the integration of doña Soledad's personality on a new level and of the creation of a new center to her personality. Furthermore, the convergence of the lines from north—symbolically the area of the unconscious—shows us the psychological source of her transformation.[93]*

The new direction is first found by Soledad lying naked in the wind, and allowing the wind to lick her body from head to toe. For

Soledad, the embarrassment of lying naked in the wind is like dying. Don Juan reveals to her that there are four winds, and that she is the north wind. The north wind is energetic, commandeering, and impatient. Soledad had been a woman who had never spoken her mind, never could reveal her fat body, and had lived without purpose. Soledad begins the arduous struggle of self-transformation and the preparation for stealing Carlos' power with the construction of the room and mandala. Through these acts Soledad has succeeded in facing a new direction, the north wind. With newfound purpose the death of the old Soledad is actuated. The ultimate triumph of the spirit, Soledad believes, will occur with overcoming Carlos and stealing his power.

Often in life it is the struggle, rather than victory or defeat, which has strengthened our spirit. In *Journey To Ixtlan* don Juan sets the stage for Carlos to do battle with la Catalina, *a worthy opponent*. When Carlos takes flight at the sight of his darkly silhouetted opponent, don Juan advises that a warrior must hold his ground:

> *"When a warrior encounters his opponent and the opponent is not an ordinary human being, he must make his stand. That is the only thing that makes him invulnerable."*
>
> *"It would be cruel if this happened to an average man," he said. "But the instant one begins to live like a warrior, one is no longer ordinary. Besides, I didn't find you a worthy opponent because I want to play with you, or tease you, or annoy you. A worthy opponent might spur you on; under the influence of an opponent like 'la Catalina' you may have to make use of everything I taught you. You don't have any other alternative."* [94]

Having to deal with a petty tyrant, or worthy opponent, is for don Juan, the opportunity of a lifetime. It is easier, but less ennobling to deal with the loving parent, rather than the challenging one. A difficult supervisor, or worthy opponent, can often provide the greatest opportunity for personal and professional growth. When we take the challenge and empower ourselves to be flexible, patient, and tolerant, we leave no room for self-pity. When we can face a new direction, and suspend judgment, we are in a position to be free of our own devices. Suspending judgment cuts through our projections and enables us to see things as they are. We can begin to see that the chains that bind us to anxiety and fear are self-constructed. Just as a psychiatrist touring the mental ward does not react personally to the barbs tossed his way, but instead considers that perhaps the patient needs different therapy or increased medication, we begin to see that we are surrounded by people who are in varying stages of growth, and our reactions are self imposed. If we have a weak or neurotic parent, spouse, child, or supervisor, we are no longer compelled to play victim. When we feel like a leaf in the wind, at the mercy of every critic who passes our way our lives are filled with reactive self-pity.

Don Juan – Losing the Human Form

Losing the human form means we no longer have a personal self to defend. We have succeeded *by using death as an advisor, to erase our personal history, and lose our self-importance.* Gorda tells Carlos how losing the human form is related to dreaming:

> *"The Nagual told me that a warrior without form begins to see an eye. I saw an eye in front of me every time I closed my eyes. It got so bad that I couldn't rest anymore; the eye followed me wherever I went. I nearly went mad. Finally, I suppose, I became used to it. Now I don't even notice it because it has become part of me."*
>
> *"The formless warrior uses that eye to start* dreaming. *If you don't have a form, you don't have to go to sleep to do* dreaming. *The eye in front of you pulls you every time you want to go."* [95]

Not having to go to sleep to do dreaming is an indication that we have gained sufficient sobriety to reside as the double. The double is that aspect of our consciousness that witnesses, but is not bound by the stream of consciousness. When we have mastered mindfulness, we are in a position to see that the witness of consciousness is the double. The witness witnesses both waking and dream state and is unchanged and unbound by either state. The warrior, having awakened in his dream, has begun to lose the human form, for to be attached to neither the waking nor dreaming state is to be formless. For Gorda, seeing an eye is her personal archetype of losing the human form. Carlos has also begun to lose his human form, but never experiences seeing an eye. In heightened states of awareness, Carlos witnesses the disintegration of the various aspects of the totality of himself as a human being, but is never really able to integrate in daily living, the tonal and the nagual in the third point of reference, the witness. Nestor, another of don Juan's disciples, who quite appropriately is nicknamed the Witness, relates how the Nagual and Genaro split Carlos:

> *"The Nagual and Genaro split you once in the eucalyptus grove. They took you there because eucalyptuses are your trees. I was there myself and I witnessed when they split you and pulled your nagual out. They pulled you apart by the ears until they had split your luminosity and you were not an egg anymore, but two long chunks of luminosity. Then they put you together again, but any sorcerer that sees can tell that there is a huge gap in the middle."* [96]

The gap in the middle of Carlos luminosity is his inability to master the third point of reference. His luminosity has been success-fully split; Genaro representing the ineffable nagual whispering in one ear, don Juan representing the warrior's tonal whispering in the other. The art of the man of knowledge is to balance the two halves of his luminosity, the tonal and the nagual, and glide fluidly between as required. Carlos is aware of both sides of his luminosity, but has not yet gained sufficient power of mindfulness and sobriety to master the third point, the witness. When he is tonal, he is all tonal; when he is nagual, he is all nagual. He indulges in both sides of his being, often giving himself up to his death when in either side. The balance of a peerless warrior comes only after years of struggle, and the victory is never final. Life is a never ending challenge for a warrior. He selects the items of his world utilizing both tonal and nagual, reason and feeling, and creates a path with heart. He is never a leaf at the mercy of the wind, but rather a peerless warrior engaging the mystery of being with wisdom and compassion.

The Ally

For those of us fortunate enough to be willing to practice training of the mind, we find deepening circles of peace, adaptation to this cycle of existence, and discerning wisdom. Discerning wisdom cuts through all the self-contracted states of mind that inhibit our inner freedom. Along the inner journey we experience the ally, don Juan's metaphor for unconscious, deeply buried archetypes, that shape our state of mind and can overwhelm our urge to self-realization. Unless we struggle with, reconcile and assimilate the silent knowledge of the ally, we cannot obtain liberation. Carl Jung, the great Swiss psychologist, and guide to the unconscious, described the invisible archetypes as inner forces:

> *Archetypes spring from a deep source that is not made by consciousness and is not under its control. In the mythology of earlier times, these forces were called mana, or spirits, demons, and gods. They are as active today as they ever were. If they conform to our wishes, we call them happy hunches or impulses and pat ourselves on the back for being smart fellows. If they go against us, then we say that it is just our bad luck, or that certain people must be against us, or that the cause of our misfortunes must be pathological, a neurosis. The one thing we refuse to admit is that we are dependent upon "powers" that are beyond our control.* [97]

Archetypes – Tara and The Black Madonna

Insight meditation cuts through the ally, the unconscious demonic archetypes that profoundly and unconsciously would inhibit our struggle towards self-realization. By struggling with the ally through meditation, and overcoming our personal and unconscious inner fears, we have the chance, perhaps for the first time in our lives, to become fully responsible for ourselves and our spiritual growth.

China Galland, in her search for the feminine goddess within, met Peter Lindegger, a philologist and Tibetologist, in Switzerland. She and Dr. Lindegger discussed Jung's archetype:

> *Jung gave the name "archetype" the myth-forming elements that seem to be present in the human psyche after he encountered variations of the same story motifs again and again in disparate cultures around the world, such as the hero who journeys into the underworld, the divine child, the enchanted princess, the Great Mother, the wise old woman or man, the evil sorcerer, and the wise fool, to name a few.*
>
> *Jung is careful to point out that an archetype is not the fact itself. These are psychic forces with their own dynamic energy found alive and operative in some form, dependent upon the culture, in every human psyche. For Jung, the archetypes were "the real but invisible roots of consciousness", threads that came up from the instinctive, primitive underworld of the collective unconscious, that vast timeless pool of human experience that seems to be transmitted in our very genes. The Great Mother, the Divine Child, the Virgin Birth, and the Dying God*

are some archetypes found in the Madonna's story and in many stories around the world, much older that Christianity's.[98]

An encounter with the ally is often marked by anxiety, fear, illness or loss of energy. Marie-Louise von Franz, a student of Jung, and an acknowledged master of Jungian psychology, discusses the loss of energy associated with meeting the ally, or the arrival of new energy from the unconscious.

> *In the individual case this is generally what we call an abaissement du niveau mental, which so often comes before an important content of the unconscious crosses the threshold of consciousness. This is partly an energetic phenomenon. Imagine that an important content, a big energetic load, is on its way up over the threshold of consciousness. When it approaches the ego complex it attracts libido from it, because, like mass particles, it has an effect upon the other particles—and this content therefore attracts libido from the ego, causing it to feel low, tired, restless, depressed, until the content breaks through.*[99]

When we are awake to our inner voices, we can take heed of their call. Our dreams, our symptoms, our intuition all point towards new found ways of being and spiritual growth. The *abaissement du niveau mental* is a manifestation of the ally, and can be assimilated into our growth by interpreting and incorporating archetypal material. We are self-empowered through our meeting with the ally when we become aware that changes in feeling or energy level can be a harbinger of constructive change.

Spiritual growth is the beginning of connecting our newfound liberation in consciousness with the circumstance of our unique life. As we grow in our mastery of awareness an inner transformation begins in which we transform dependency and egoic confusion into transcending awareness, self-empowerment, and compassion.

For don Juan, the third enemy of a man of knowledge is knowledge itself. When we become bound to the training, or the spiritual master, or even the path itself, our subtle clinging is the impediment to all-encompassing enlightenment. Beyond the veil of knowledge we surrender to the pathless path, to the sacred mystery of our eternal and momentary being, to the light of divine love-bliss. We take our place in the infinite and numinous Buddha fields, and empower all with eyes to see, and ears to hear, with the all pervading, now radiant, luminous spirit of self-transcendence.

8. THE PURPOSE OF MEDITATION

Metamorphosis

Although western man often views his spiritual salvation through strict adherence to doctrine as set forth by the leaders of his particular religious denomination, the esoteric teachings of Buddhism, Hinduism, and Christianity point towards modes of realization beyond dogma. The great sage Saraha said:

> Alas, a yogin who has realized the innate simplicity of mind
> And who still carries on with formal religious practices
> Is like someone who has discovered a precious gem
> But who still searches for an ordinary stone.
> However much he may strive,
> His practice is devoid of essence.[100]

The path to spiritual growth in these esoteric teachings occurs in the here and now, although it is believed in the Eastern traditions, that growth may continue during many lifetimes. The means for appropriating esoteric knowledge comes about through analytical investigation and fixed attentiveness. What is to be analyzed is the nature of mind, and what is to be concurrently practiced is the stabilization of attentiveness.

Why is all of this necessary, and what can be accomplished? The object of meditation is to achieve liberation from *samsara*, illusions of the discursive mind. We are not seeking to negate conventional knowledge; where we live, how to build a house, travel to a distant city, etc. We are seeking the next stage in our psychological growth; a stage of growth beyond that which is normally perceived in the west as adulthood. Our level of adulthood, utilizing higher stage Buddhist and Hindu teachings as a benchmark, is a case of arrested development. The late Haridas Chaudhuri, professor of philosophy and president of the California Institute of Asian Studies, commented sagely on the stages of growth:

> In the Taittiriya Upanishad, it is shown how as a spiritual seeker grows and evolves to higher and higher levels of self-awareness, his metaphysical world view begins to change in a corresponding manner. When a person is completely identified with the body he looks upon the

world as an extension of his body. He is predominantly a materialist in outlook, and affirms matter as the creative source of all existence. When a person is identified with his life force, he looks upon the universe as the flux of vital energy. In other words, he is predominantly a vitalist in outlook and affirms life as the creative source of all existence. When he identifies with pure reason, he becomes an objective idealist in philosophy and affirms reason as the creative source of all existence. When he identifies with his pure transcendental awareness, which is a blissful experience, he becomes a mystic-seer or spiritual idealist in outlook, and affirms existence-consciousness-bliss as the creative source of all existence. When finally he identifies with pure indeterminable Being or Nothingness, he becomes a transcendental ontologist like Buddha (the founder of Buddhism) and Samkara (the most-well known exponent of Vedanta), and affirms Nothingness or indeterminable Being as the ultimate ground of existence.[101]

Continuing even further beyond Nothingness or indeterminable Being is a possibility explored in this book, as exemplified by the spiritual realizations of the Mahamudra, Dzogpa Chenpo, and Adi Da. Growth in consciousness is especially difficult in a society without genuine spiritual rites of passage, or widely available esoteric masters, but not impossible. The flowering, or illumination we seek is a necessity for living one's life in harmony and mental equilibrium. A transformation in consciousness is brought about by an awakening into the nondual nature and nonselfhood of awareness. This transformation is nothing less than a mystical encounter with the spirit, relinquishment of the traditional egoic self, and metamorphosis into a flexible, highly adapted man or woman of knowledge and numinous being.

Tranquility

It is essential for the beginner in meditation to deepen his mastery of tranquility through the stabilization of attention. Insight is developed and deepens as the meditator explores the nature of reality. This exploration into insight must be enacted concurrent with meditative absorption. Without learning how to pacify the turbulent stirring of mind, through analytic examination while in meditative equipoise, one's psychoneurotic excursions will not be eliminated. Tranquility and insight are inseparable components. Their mastery will eventually lead to transcendental wisdom, and the awakening of the spiritual self.

Adi Da – Thinking Is A Way In, Not A Way Out

The first, and most important aspect of tranquility is settling the mind. We must be willing to disengage from our habitual concern with the preoccupations of everyday life. If we cannot disengage from our emotional attachments, and our internal dialog, we will not be able to settle the mind. The neurotic mind gives up its control very slowly and cautiously, if at all. The neurotic mind tells itself that there is nothing beyond that which the neurotic mind knows, and to practice tranquility can only bring boredom. The neurotic mind deceives itself, despite continuing and pervasive evidence to the contrary that the solution to wellness of mind can be found through further internal chatter, or external dialogue with well meaning professional healers who may be no more sound of mind than their neurotic patients.[102] Meditation is not indicated for the severely maladjusted personality. Deep rooted psychological trauma, psychosis, and personality disorders can be addressed by appropriate psychotherapies, perhaps in combination with relaxation techniques. When there is sufficient wellness of being and self-integration the practice of meditation can begin. Adi Da clarifies the nature of apparent bondage:

> *Thinking Is A Way In, Not A Way Out. You Cannot (Ever or Possibly) <u>think</u> Your Way Out Of the Apparent Bondage (or Apparent Problem) That Is conditional Existence, but You, By Most Of Your thinking, Are Tending To Constantly Re-Affirm and Re-Assert Your bondage and Your Problems.*
>
> *Any and every kind of thinking Is Necessarily a conditional activity, and Therefore, thinking Cannot (itself) Eliminate or Transcend conditional Existence (Itself).*
>
> *The Only Process That Is Able To Eliminate or Transcend The Apparent Bondage (or Apparent Problem) That Is conditional Existence Is One That Inherently and Most Priorly Transcends (or Stands, Inherently, and Inherently Most Perfectly, Prior To) conditional Existence.*
>
> *Apart From Such A Process (Which Is Inherently Perfect and Inherently Free), thinking <u>Never</u> Leads Out Of Bondage (and, Thus, To Freedom), but thinking (Unless it Is Simply An Extension, and An Expression, or An Otherwise Effective Servant, Of The Inherently*

*Perfect Realization Of Prior Freedom) Always leads Further and
Further Into Bondage Itself (and Every Kind Of conceived or Otherwise
Presumed Problem).*[103]

The root of neurotic or non-pathological unhappiness is the non-stop chatter of mind. To seek relief through the source of suffering is ultimately unsuccessful and absurd. Although this circular path rarely leads to final release from neurotic suffering, the neurotic mind is stubbornly unwilling to let go of its self-inflicted obsessions, delusions, and maladaptive behaviors. The neurotic mind grinds ever deeper and deeper into its own self-made rut, looking everywhere for release, excluding the one possibility where the end of suffering is to be found—silence and the guru within.

Conditions Necessary For Mastering Tranquility

There are certain conditions necessary to begin the meditation on tranquility. Most of us have experienced profound moments of tranquility, but very few of us know how to experience tranquil mind at will. Without mastering tranquility, each and every moment is defined by inner dialogue or apparent outside circumstance. If we are serious in our intent to begin a new way of being in this life we must appropriate new skills. The beginning of the way to appropriate the mastery of mind is through the mastery of tranquility. The place set aside for meditation should be quiet, a place where there is little occasion for disturbance by outside noise or interference by other people. Meditation is a practice mastered in solitude. If we are unable to abandon input or stimulus causing mental and physical distraction, we will be unable to abandon the wanderings of mind and realize tranquility.

Physical Position and Behavior

After having established a personal place for meditation the meditation session should begin with an appropriate physical posture. If the body is not balanced in alignment, physical discomfort will overcome the ability to concentrate. Although one can eventually overcome uncomfortable meditation positions, my feeling is that while physical position is important, it is not necessary that everyone adopt the same posture. If you are comfortable sitting

in the traditional Buddhist meditation position that I will describe—
fine; if not—find your own!

In the vajra, or Buddha posture, the meditator assumes the
following:

1. Sitting cross-legged on a soft cushion in the traditional
   Buddha position.

2. The hands are placed close to the abdomen, with the
   back of the left hand is in the palm of the right hand,
   both palms facing up, and the two thumbs resting
   against each other.

3. The backbone is straight, so that the whole body is
   secure and comfortable.

4. Arms and elbows are hanging straight down from the
   shoulders and relaxed.

5. The chin is slightly bent down towards the neck.

6. Lips are lightly closed, with the tongue lightly
   touching the upper palate. The teeth are just lightly
   touching.

7. The eyes are set in a fixed gaze just beyond the tip of
   the nose.

It has been observed that by adopting this posture the energy
circulating in the body is revitalized, and that tranquil absorption
will arise naturally as the discursive mind is pacified. Furthermore,
the mind will not be overcome by dullness or emotional discrimination. Clarity of mind will become manifest.

The most difficult part of beginning a program of meditation is
the beginning. The discursive mind will not give up its control
easily. While very young children can sit for hours in quiet non-
verbal play, by the time we are adults the thought of sitting quietly
without internal chatter is nearly impossible. It is this internal chatter
that we are seeking to overcome, so that we may gain access to the
mind and its eventual mastery. I cannot emphasize enough that the
way to sanity and spiritual growth is not through continuing our

past practice of giving free reign to our internal dialogue, but in mastering awareness. This can only come about through mastering silence. It is not that we are thereafter going to lead a life of silence, but that we will no longer allow ourselves to be defined by the relentless stream of internal chatter. We will no longer drive down the highway of life as though our hands are on the rear view mirror, rather than the steering wheel. With mastery of mind we will be free to pursue our interests, with clarity, wisdom and love. We will listen more thoroughly, understand more deeply and compassionately, and live and love in sanity and peace.

Bhagawan Rajneesh – Mirror Meditation

An extremely powerful meditation operates on the principle of the stabilization of consciousness through biological feedback. It is a method utilizing a mirror, with feedback occurring between consciousness and minute scanning movement of the eyes.

Bhagawan Shree Rajneesh, in his excellent, *Meditation: The Art of Ecstasy*, describes the method as follows:

> *At night before you go to bed, close the doors of your room and put a big mirror in front of you. The room must be completely dark. Then put a small flame by the side of the mirror in such a way that the flame is not directly reflected in the mirror. Just your face should be reflected in the mirror, not the flame.*
>
> *Stare constantly into your own eyes in the mirror. Do not blink. This is a forty minute experiment, and within two or three days you will be able to keep your eyes from blinking for the whole forty minutes. Even if tears come, let them come. But, still, do not blink, and go on staring into the eyes.*
>
> *Within two or three days you will become aware of a very strange phenomenon: your face will begin to take on new shapes. You may even be scared! The face in the mirror will begin to change. Sometimes a very different face will be there—one which you have not known to be yours, but all the faces that come to you belong to you. Now the subconscious mind is beginning to explode. These faces, these masks, are yours. And sometimes you may even see a face that belonged to you in a past life.*
>
> *After one week of constant practice—staring for forty minutes every night—your face will be a constant flux. Many faces will be coming and going constantly. After three weeks you will not be able to remember which one is your face. You will not be able to remember your own face because you have seen so many different faces coming and*

going.

If you continue, then one day—after three weeks or so—the strangest thing will happen: suddenly there will be no face in the mirror. The mirror will be vacant. You are staring into emptiness; there will be no face at all.

This is the moment! Close your eyes, and encounter the unconscious. When there is no face in the mirror, just close the eyes. This is the most significant moment. Close the eyes, look inside, and you will face the unconscious. You will be naked, completely naked—as you are. All deceptions will fall.[104]

The point is not to get hung up on method, or psychic phenomenon. What we are after is not strange faces or visions of flashing lights, but rather, the harnessing of consciousness into a more tractable and wise mode of operation. We have spent most of our lives living in our thoughts, with little separation between thought and naked *being.* That is, just *being,* without the incessant inner voice defining, judging, discerning, and otherwise obscuring our moment-to-moment awareness.

Counting The Breath Meditation

Another powerful meditation for achieving tranquil absorption is to count breaths. The meditator settles comfortably in his meditation position and focuses his concentration on the inward and outward movement of the breath, through the nostrils, while counting. He can begin by counting up to ten or twenty and eventually work his way up to a hundred, or higher.

The Nine Stages of Mental Abiding

One: Settling The Mind

In order to settle the mind the mind focuses on a selected object with mindfulness, and maintains the chosen image. Mindfulness is being cognizant of the selected object without being forgetful. The selected object must be one that is totally familiar to the meditator. There must be single-pointed concentration on the object without distraction. The mind is completely withdrawn from external phenomena.

Two: Maintaining Concentration

The meditator must instantly recognize excursions of thought and return awareness to the object of meditation. Being overcome by either dullness or excitement will cause the focus of meditation to drift. Meditation sessions should be kept short so that the meditator will become familiar with maintaining concentration and not be overcome by either dullness or excitement. In this way the meditator will gain experience with maintaining the concentrated state of mind. Just as in learning how to drive, the concentration required at first is considerable, but later, driving becomes second nature. With familiarity, practice, and maintaining concentration for longer periods of time while guarding against excursions of mind and dullness or excitement, concentration will become effortless.

Three: Revitalizing The Concentration

The meditator becomes increasingly familiar with the settled state of mind and revitalizes his concentration by redirecting excursions of thought back to the object of meditation, and the settled state of mind. Absent-mindfulness and wandering thoughts are quickly observed and the mind is settled deeper and deeper into the concentration. The meditator, having become familiar with the settled state of awareness, can now much more readily observe divergence and revitalize the concentration.

Four: Firmly Settled Concentration

The meditator has finally become aware of the power of mind-fulness. Vigilant mindfulness can detect the emergence of coarse and subtle thoughts, and redirect awareness towards the firmly settled state. He can still be overcome by dullness, excitement, or forgetfulness, and may have to either increase or decrease his effort to achieve the settled state. Just as the ripples from a stone dropped into still water gradually settle, concentration pervades the mind.

Five: Mastery Of Concentration

Comparable to the Eskimo who has more than fifty words to describe snow, the meditator through inner development, has become familiar with already existent, but previously hidden mental states. The virtues of tranquility and the mastery of concentration are beginning to be appreciated. Disciplining the mind, and overcoming dullness, mental excitement, and forgetfulness are still required; however, the virtues of meditation have become much more readily apparent. The meditator is becoming increasingly aware that something exciting is happening.

Six: Pacification Of Excitement

As the abiding nature of mind becomes more apparent, excitement increases. This creates the requirement to pacify the mind and overcome the subtle excitement of the fifth mental abiding. Through the application of subtle introspection, dullness and excitement are successfully overcome. The power of vigilant mindfulness has become a sharply honed tool in the arsenal of concentration.

Seven: Total Pacification Of Mental Stains

The meditator is increasingly aware of the emotional afflictions arising in the mind. He can now, through the coating of mindfulness, pacify anxiety, lust, worry, drowsiness, and other mental stains. He is able to discern the moment defilement arises in consciousness and apply vigilant mindfulness to settle the mind in tranquil concentration. The meditator must still rely on effort to restore the seventh mental abiding, having not yet gained the skill to ride the wave of mind effortlessly. He has, however, become aware that through further practice he will be able to sustain the concentrated state of mind constantly and without effort.

Eight: One-Pointed Concentration

Having attained the ability to totally pacify mental stains, dullness and excitement can no longer overpower the eighth mental abiding. With an almost effortless push the meditator enters the state of tranquil concentration, and is able to maintain this state for the entire meditation session. His attainment is now constant and effortless. Application of antidotes would be a fault as dullness and excitement are no longer features of the one-pointed concentration. The meditator remains tranquilly absorbed abiding in effortless equanimity. The power of effort has matured into effortless, unstained mental abiding.

Nine: Settling In Tranquil Equipoise

The mastery of the one-pointed concentration results in effortless, spontaneous, mental stabilization. The meditator, without effort, enters and resides in the tranquil absorption. The Prajnaparamita-sacayagatha states:

> Strive to achieve tranquil absorption
> Through uninterrupted contemplation
> On inner purity.
> Just as the striking of two flints
> With long pauses in between
> Will not cause sparks,
> So occasional meditation
> Will not lead to tranquility .
> Do not give up until perfection is achieved! [105]

Recognizing Flawless Meditation

After much practice, perfect absorptive tranquility is attained. The mind in this state is serenely stable, like the image of the Buddha in repose. The resultant mind rests with serenity and lucidity and is clear like space. One realizes the mind to be without center or circumference, and to be an unceasing stream of clarity and emptiness. With further practice and the emergence of insight, the meditator will be able to maintain this state nearly indefinitely and will begin to perfect the first of four stages of yoga; the one-pointed stage. The second Bhavanakrama states:

> Thus, by concentrating on a visualized image of one's choice the meditator should continuously focus on it. Having done so perfectly, he should examine if the concentrating mind has a firm grip of the visualized image, if it is being clouded with dullness, or if it is wandering toward external objects, thus being distracted.[106]

Heart Master Adi Da advises the following:

> In This Manner, Instead Of Following thoughts and sensations themselves (and Thus Merely Observing and Submitting To their Potential permutations or results), Always Trace thoughts and sensations To

their Mysteriously "Objective" (and Yet Formless, Imageless, and Soundless) Point and Space Of Origin Above.

The Primary Intention and Purpose Of Ascending Meditation Is To Transcend thoughts and sensations (or all of the conditional movements and objects of attention) By Contemplating (or Submitting attention To) the Place, Source, Carrier, Current, or Matrix In Which thoughts and sensations Are arising.

Freely Allow thoughts and sensations to arise, but Do Not Passively Indulge In them.[107]

Requirements For Mastering Tranquility

In order to master tranquility there are four mental properties required.

> 1. An initial effort at the beginning of each meditation session is required to produce tranquil absorption.
>
> 2. When dullness or thought flow interrupts absorption, intermittent effort is required to reassert absorption.
>
> 3. An effortless awareness is required to maintain absorption when concentration is not being interrupted by dullness or thought flow.
>
> 4. A spontaneous awareness is attained when tranquility is effortlessly achieved.

There are many meditations suitable for developing powerful absorption. Although one may adopt the lotus position for meditation, a commonly known posture with all of the limbs and trunk of the body in precise yogic balance, I did not. I did, however, seat myself in the most comfortable upholstered chair I possessed, and adopted my most stable and relaxed position. I found a time in the late evening when I would not be disturbed, either by telephone calls, noises within the house, or street noises. I then proceeded to consider the question, "Who am I"?

As you ask this question of yourself, you first define yourself by the most obvious. I am the child of my parents and was named by them. You inquire, "Who were my parents, and my parents' parents," ad infinitum. Seeing that there is no definitive answer along this branch of thought you try another. You may consider—I am a person, and just what is a person? How do I differ from other people? How am I significantly different from the billions of other people on this planet? Who are they? What are we all doing here? In fact, where is the *here* I am thinking of? Does the *here* exist without my being *here* to label it? Am I more than the fusion of a sperm and egg? What is a sperm or egg ultimately? How does genetic material come into existence? Does existence exist independent of an observer? What does observerless existence look like? If existence doesn't exist without me, do I exist without existence? Does existence exist? You continue session after session, in the manner of a Zen koan, until you come to the end. At that moment, if this is a suitable method for you, you will know who you are in the most profound way possible. You will also have been somewhat successful in your first glimpse of the one-pointed yoga.

9. MEDITATION ON THE SELF

Don Juan – Stopping The World

There cannot be lasting tranquility without mindfulness. Mindfulness redirects the discursive mind towards one-pointed stabilization. One-pointed stabilization empowers insight. Mystic awareness is available to each of us when our own true nature is not obscured by the inner dialogue, and awareness is not contracted within mind into an egoic self. In *Tales of Power*, Carlos Castaneda describes to the Yaqui Indian man of knowledge, don Juan, how quieting the mind first affected him. Carlos had been instructed by don Juan to practice walking for long stretches without focusing his eyes on anything, a technique to facilitate stopping the internal dialogue.

> *I told don Juan I had practiced the technique for years without noticing any change, but I had expected none anyway. One day, however, I had the shocking realization that I had just walked for about ten minutes without having said a single word to myself.*
>
> *I mentioned to don Juan that on the occasion I also became cognizant that stopping the internal dialogue involved more than merely curtailing the words I said to myself. My entire thought processes had stopped and I had felt I was practically suspended, floating. A sensation of panic had ensued from that awareness and I had to resume my internal dialogue as an antidote.[108]*

Hubert Benoit – The Zen Of Mind

It is most important to explore this sense of panic. Hubert Benoit, in his penetrating psychological survey of the Zen of mind, *The Supreme Doctrine*, relates how floating free beyond time and space and returning to absolute subjectivity, panics the consciousness explorer.

> *Suddenly he becomes conscious that his principle is not the principle of the universe, that there are things that exist independently of him, he becomes conscious of it in suffering from contact with the world-obstacle. At this moment appears conscious fear of death, of the danger which the Not-Self represents for the self.[109]*

Ken Wilber – Unity Of Life And Death

Ken Wilber in his masterful and encyclopedic tour of mind, *The Spectrum of Consciousness*, discusses the difficulty of grasping the unity of life and death:

> *The fact that life and death are "not two" is extremely difficult for most individuals to grasp, and the difficulty lies not in the direction of complexity but rather of simplicity—it is not too complex to understand, it is rather too simple, so that we miss it at the very point where we begin to think about it. Life is ordinarily taken to be something that begins at birth and ends at death, so that life and birth are irreconcilably set against death. But in actuality, life and death, or more appropriately, birth and death, are nothing but two different ways of viewing the reality of the present Moment. As we have seen, in the absolute Present there is no past, and that which has no past is something which is just born. Birth is the condition of having no past. Further, in the absolute Present there is no future either, and that which has no future is something which has just died. Death is the condition of having no future. Thus the present Moment, because it has no future, it is simultaneously dead. Birth and death, therefore, are simply two ways of talking about the same timeless Moment, and they are illusorily separated only by those "who cannot escape from the standpoint of temporal succession so as to see all things in their simultaneity." In short, birth and death are one in this timeless Moment.[110]*

Don Juan – Losing The Human Form

For Gorda, in *The Second Ring Of Power*, becoming aware of the death of the egoic self is losing the human form. Through mastery of the *not-doing* of the self, and stopping the inner dialogue, the world stops. If the warrior does not become physically sick he may even go insane as a result of his direct contact with the nagual:

> *He (don Juan) said that some part of us is always kept under lock and key because we are afraid of it, and that to our reason, that part of us was like an insane relative that we kept in a locked dungeon. That part, was in La Gorda's terms, our second attention, and when it finally could focus on something the world stopped. Since we, as average men, know only the attention of the tonal, it is not too farfetched to say that once attention is canceled, the world has to stop. The focusing of our wild, untrained second attention has to be, perforce, terrifying. Don Juan was right in saying that the only way to keep our insane relative from*

bursting in on us was by shielding ourselves with our endless internal dialog.[111]

Unbending intent, sobriety, and repeated contact with the nagual over extended periods of time, begins to balance the two sides of the warrior, the tonal and the nagual. For most of us on the path of inner growth, this is a life long struggle. If we rely too heavily on the tonal, we become unbalanced by the weight of the demands of our every-day world. If we become lost in the mysterious nagual, the side of silent knowledge, we may never return. For Gorda, physical illness was a consequence of losing the human form. Carlos describes Gorda's experience of the nagual:

She then described a very complex series of sensations that she had had over a period of years that culminated in a serious illness, the climax of which was a bodily state that reminded me of descriptions I had read of a massive heart attack. She said that the human form, as the force that it is, left her body after a serious internal battle that manifested itself as illness.[112]

When faced with losing the human form, no matter how the individual manifestation occurs, many meditators bow out of any further practice. Sheer terror seizes the meditator as he faces the abyss of seeming self-annihilation. For if time and space and the con-cept of self exist only in consciousness, then the meditator mis-takenly believes that he is staring at his own death. He is, however, standing on a metaphysical tightrope:

"What happens to the persons whose assemblage points loses rigidity?" I asked.
"If they're not warriors, they think they're losing their minds," he said smiling. "Just as you thought you were going crazy at one time."
"If they're warriors, they know they've gone crazy, but they patiently wait. You see, to be healthy and sane means that the assemblage point is immovable. When it shifts, it literally means that one is deranged."[113]

Nagarjuna – Self-Nature

The impeccable warrior sees that there is no self to be found; nor on the other hand, a self who can die. Nagarjuna makes the following assertion:

Without self-nature and other-nature, whence can there be an existent? For the existent is established only when there is self-nature or other-nature.[114]

Nagarjuna is making the point that having no self-nature precludes existents. The predication of a self-nature without other-nature could not establish a point of reference for self-nature. If other-nature is not established on its own side, then neither can self-nature be established. Another example might be to imagine an awareness in the emptiness of deep space without any surrounding objects. By what means could this awareness be self-referential. There would be no means of establishing its own size, weight, color, smell, etc., because all of these units are learned constructions in consciousness utilizing relative comparison. The illusion of self-nature requires awareness functioning within a field of apparent other objects and within the apparent three periods of time, arising unobstructed in union with emptiness. The first Bhavanakrama elaborates:

Thus, one contemplates that the three planes of phenomenal existence are the product of mind only, and then one realizes that everything conceptually designated is simply of mental origin. If one examines every aspect of the mind, one is analyzing the intrinsic nature of all phenomena. In so examining one may further examine in the following manner. The mind as such cannot be real from the standpoint of ultimate truth. How can mind be real when it clings to images of what are essentially false sensory forms, etc., manifesting themselves externally in diverse appearances? Just as sensory forms, etc. are false, so the mind is also false since it is not any different from the former. The senses—emerging in diverse forms—are devoid of either one or many essences. The reality of the mind is not different from the senses; it is also devoid of either one or many essences. For these reasons the mind by nature is indeed like a magical scene. Like the mind, all phenomena in their intrinsic nature are also like a magical scene.[115]

The three periods of time, past, present, and future, as well as exterior objects, do not exist in their own right. Nagarjuna is saying that existents are appearances in consciousness and empty of essence. Birth and death, as well, are in union with appearance and emptiness, and are non-veridical on their own side. From the point of view of the witness of consciousness, since birth and death, past, present and future, self and others, arise as appearances in awareness in union with emptiness, we can neither establish their existence nor non-existence. The Flower Ornament Scripture says:

> Of past, present, and future times,
> Understanding all that's said,
> Yet knowing all times are equal:
> This is the power of skill of incomparable understanding.[116]

The Samdhivyakarana-sutra comments:

> Concerning the definitive meaning of the enlightened mind,
> One has to ascertain it repeatedly.
> Such a mind is neither within nor without, nor both.
> It is neither mutable, nor eternal, nor momentary,
> For it is self-cognizing awareness.[117]

Je Phagmo Trupa defines the nondual, self-cognizing awareness as Mahamudra:

> Mahamudra means nondual [awareness].
> Its three aspects are
> Essence, nature, and characteristics.
> "Essence" means the emptiness
> Of arising, ceasing, or conceiving.
> "Nature" means unobstructed lucidity.
> "Characteristics" mean the diverse appearances
> On the levels of samsara and nirvana.[118]

The Mahamudratilaka gives the Tibetan Buddhist equivalent of *mahamudra*—Chakgya Chenpo:

> As regards the chakgya chenpo,
> Chak stands for awareness of vacuity [sunyata],
> Gya signifies its intrinsic quality that transcends existential duality,
> Chenpo symbolizes the union of the two.[119]

The significance of this for the meditator at this stage, is the observation the he is the witness of consciousness. The self-cognizing awareness of the observer has three aspects: emptiness, lucidity, and diverse appearances. Upon what basis is the viewer of this nondual continuum to be imputed? If there is no inherent validity to all that surrounds us—then how can the inherent nature of the viewer be asserted? Everything perceived by the meditator has only relative being; neither tall nor short, separate nor together, pervious nor impervious. Nothing can be asserted about the meditator with absolute or non-relative distinction. The meditator witnesses the union of co-dependently arising appearance and emptiness. He is directly facing the nagual. If he chooses to continue on the path of knowledge he is faced with a long and difficult task of integrating the social and the numinous side of his being into one luminous whole, the totality of himself. He will eventually participate in the apparent world from neither vantage point exclusively. The man of knowledge can effortlessly glide between the tonal and the nagual, and assemble the world empowered with wisdom and compassion. Don Juan relates the enormity of this possibility and advises Carlos that the seer, having broken the barrier of perception, discovers the inherent freedom of awareness:

> "To assemble other worlds is not only a matter of practice, but a matter of intent," he continued. "And it isn't merely an exercise of bouncing out of those worlds, like being pulled by a rubber band. You see, a seer has to be daring. Once you break the barrier of perception, you don't have to come back to the same place in the world. See what I mean?" [120]

The Ajna Door – Crack Between The Worlds

At first, the passage to the nagual appears as a crack between the worlds, in Adi Da's terminology the ajna door. Through unrelenting intent, and the practice of various *not-doings*, the tonal begins to give up its powerful hold. In the world of don Juan, breaking the hold of the tonal through *not-doing* is a key factor. The *not-doing* of being allows us to see that the world is held together by the alignment of the assemblage point. The assemblage point is the focus of awareness upon selected emanations. Our awareness selects internal and external emanations to align the particular world we perceive. Once our awareness becomes fixed upon the place on the specific spot on the luminous cocoon of awareness via our internal dialog, a sophisticated maneuver is required to move the assemblage point. For don Juan, petty tyrants or worthy opponents are aids in helping to move the assemblage point. Perceiving the ally (unconscious representations of the spirit which manifest themselves as images, instincts, hunches, or emotional drives) is an indication that the apprentice has moved his assemblage point from its customary position. He has succeeded in breaking the bonds of self-reflection. For the apprentice or meditator, the transcendental self must be reached by stopping the internal dialogue, concentrating upon and mastering attention, and reaching the place of silent being. For don Juan, dreaming is a means of stabilizing attention. The warrior who is able to wake up in his dream and find his hands, look away and find his hands again, has become sober in his waking life, and awake in his sleeping life. Through practicing with greater and greater mindfulness in his daily life, the warrior, with unbending intent, is able to focus attention, whether asleep or awake, as the witness of consciousness, rather than as the content of consciousness:

> *"The Nagual told us to show you that with our attention we can hold images of a dream in the same way we hold the images of the world," la Gorda said. "The art of the dreamer is the art of attention."* [121]

The warrior arrives at a critical juncture. He sees that the experience of dreaming is no more 'real' than the experience of being 'awake'. He has found his double. His double is the awareness of himself as the witness of all and the apparent experiencer of all. He sees or feels the lines of the world emanating as structures in consciousness. As a nagual he upholds the manifestation with feeling. As a tonal he upholds the world through talk. Neither has more weight than the other. The warrior exercises controlled folly to restore and live in the world, and chooses a path with heart.

Along the way the warrior struggles with the ally. Every warrior manifests the ally in a manner unique to himself. The allies, or archetypes, are subconscious forces that are either overcome by a warrior on the path of knowledge, or bring about his downfall. The ally may manifest itself in vision, or psychosomatic eruption. Without having this inner struggle we would be unable to become self-actualized. Being born into a perfectly stressless existence, with every want instantly satisfied, would leave us without challenge. The challenge of the warrior is to overcome and assimilate his ally, self-empowered through the mastery of awareness.

Beyond The Ajna Door - The Witness

In *The Second Ring of Power*, Carlos Castaneda faces formidable opponents in a life and death encounter. Don Juan, prior to having left this world, instructed the female warriors of Carlos' cycle to encounter Carlos in a struggle to the death. Carlos meets his opponents and behaves in his habitually weak ways. Soledad, Gorda, Lidia, Rosa, and Josephina seek to overwhelm Carlos and steal his luminosity. When we have the opportunity in life to struggle with a formidable opponent, or petty tyrant, we can either ennoble our spirit and ourselves, or die. As Carlos battles, and is on the brink of extinction, his spirit breaks the boundaries of the tonal, releasing the instinctively manifested power of the nagual and defeating his would be assassins. Carlos victory foreshadows the arrival of a fully self-empowered man of knowledge. Carlos does not yet, however, have the personal power to sustain and balance the two halves of his luminosity, and almost immediately reverts to all tonal. He is unable to self-validate victory, and seeks confirmation through explanation as to what had happened. Until Carlos can assimilate silent knowledge as power, he will have a hole in his luminosity. Gorda tells Carlos:

> "I should tell you.... that you have to remember your bouts with Soledad and the little sisters and examine every single thing that happened to you with them, because everything is an omen of what will happen to you on your path. If you are careful and impeccable, you'll find that those bouts were gifts of power." [122]

> "Now you're a warrior with two faces," she went on. "The Nagual said that all of us have to have two faces to fare well in both attentions. He and Genaro helped us to round up our second attention and turned us around so we could face in two directions, but they didn't help you, because to be a true nagual you have to claim your power all by yourself. You're still a long way from that, but let's say that now you're walking upright instead of crawling, and when you've regained your completeness and have lost your form, you'll be gliding." [123]

The meditator may be unable to make any further distinction regarding the nature of his actions or existence, and at this point in his development is advised to relax while neither seeking nor clinging. Nagarjuna, choosing the middle path, indicates that it is wisest not to attempt to clarify that which is beyond knowing:

> "Exists" implies grasping after eternalism. "Does not exist" implies the philosophy of annihilation. Therefore, a discerning person should not rely upon either existence or non-existence. [124]

The Lankavatara-sutra further states:

Do not conceive external reality
Through the inference of the mind.
Focus your mind on the suchness of emptiness
And then transcend the mind itself!
Settle the mind in the emptiness of appearance
By transcending the phenomena of appearance.
A yogin who has settled his mind in the emptiness of appearance
Will indeed see the Mahayana.[125]

Je Yanggonpa advises not to attempt any further reduction by analyzing that which transcends the mind:

Do not let your undistracted mindfulness lose its focus;
Do not modify or meditate on the abiding nature of phenomena;
Do not desire to define that which transcends the mind;
Do not distort it by investigation
Maintain this state openly!
You will unify the meditation on and attainment of
The nondiscriminatory yoga,
Like the reunion of a mother and her only daughter.[126]

If one can go beyond the state of self induced terror only purity is found. The first Bhavanakrama states:

Meditate upon the nonselfhood of all things, which are comprised of the five psychological aggregates, the twelve sense formations, and the eighteen realms of the elements. Ultimately, apart from being manifestations of the mind, these aggregate, sense formations, and elements do not have an independent reality. No object of attachment can exist, as the essence of reality itself is nonexistent. Their reduction to particles and finally to infinitesimal proportions will show this. Determining reality in this manner, one should contemplate that from beginingless time, due to their deep clinging to the apparent reality of phenomena, childish sentient beings have mistaken the mind's manifestations for external reality in much the same way a dreamer holds his dreams to be true. Ultimately, all these are but manifestations of the mind.[127]

Adi Da describes the ajna door, as potentially being the ajna knot, which obscures the seeing of the witness of consciousness:

Until The Ajna Door Is Fully Opened (or Otherwise Fully Transcended By Native Identification With The Witness-Position Of Consciousness), It Is Truly, the Ajna Knot. Un-Opened (or Not Otherwise Tran-

scended), the Ajna Door (or Ajna Knot) Functions As A Stress-Point That (Apparently) Confines Self-Radiant (or Inherently Spiritual) and Transcendental (or Self-Existing) and, Ultimately, Divine Being to subtle, and Even gross, conditional Patterns Of egoity (By Confining the Spirit-Current and attention To the subtle, and Even gross, fields of brain and/or mind).[128]

The Mahamudra meditator unites tranquility and insight, while cultivating no seeking, no clinging, and nondual awareness:

The central insights here are as follows. First, one aims to dissolve the division of meditation and meditator, realizing them as inseparable union without any essence. Second, one examines again the destination of past thought, the nature of present thought, and the source of future thought, until one comes to the conviction that these thoughts are not assignable to the three times and are uniquely pure and open, for all times. Third, one tries to dissolve any residual dualities between "internal" and "external", "subject" and "object", so that all experience is seen as a single stream, self-emerging and self-releasing.[129]

It is important to consolidate and test the gains made during meditation by extending the elevated awareness to post-meditation experience. The petty tyrant, or formidable opponent of don Juan, as well as stressful circumstances of daily living can provide the apparently negative and adverse conditions with which the meditator can elevate or sublimate his awareness. Strong faith is an additional requisite. The Mahamudra meditator is on the path of spiritual blessing. The meditator will come to know that he is indivisible with the underlying ground of being.

10. INSIGHT

Conceptual Designations

When we view a tree, we perceive brown bark, green leaves, etc. Our perception is constructed through our visual apparatus, in conjunction with received light radiation bouncing off the tree. We are not directly in contact with the object of our perception. Rather, we receive the signal once removed from the object through bounced radiation. If we could, in some way momentarily be the tree, and get under its bark, so to speak, it is apparent that we would not perceive brown bark or green leaves. A tree, obviously, does not have visual apparatus to see color as we do. The brown and green are not inherent aspects, or self-knowledge of the tree. Brown and green arise within our consciousness as a result of the presence of the field of the tree, light, and the tree being within the range of our field of perception. Brown and green are not aspects of the tree, just as sweetness is not an aspect of sugar from its own side. Nagarjuna explains how the coemergence of emptiness and the coemergence of appearance are indivisible:

> By their self-nature rock-sugar is sweet
> And fire is hot;
> So the intrinsic nature of all things
> Is said to be empty [of substance].[130]

Rock-sugar, if it were to have a self-nature, would be immersed in the sensation of sweetness. Fire, likewise, if it were to have a self-nature, would be experiencing heat. Rock-sugar has no sweetness as an aspect of its own side; the sweetness is a characteristic of our taste sense. Fire does not perceive its own warmth; the heat of fire is an aspect of our sensory apparatus perceiving the fires radiation and creating meaning through repeated sensory stimulation. Fire does not perceive heat on its own side. Likewise, you as the possessor of a face cannot perceive the appearance of your face. Others impute a relative appearance—which is in union with emptiness. All things are said to be empty of substance because attributes do not exist on their own side as qualities of self-nature. Nagarjuna affirms the unity of appearance and emptiness:

Apparent reality is stated to be empty;
Emptiness means apparent reality,
For their mutual nonexclusion is a certainty,
Like the interrelatedness between the conditioned
          and their transitory nature.[131]

Of equal importance is the consideration of you, the perceiver, as a separate self. Your existence is a codependent arising. Your apparent self is empty of one or many essences. Your sense of self is coemergent with the perceptions of the five senses. The five senses are indivisibly united in the emptiness of the coemergent mind and coemergent appearance. Virupa sums up:

Thus all apparent things that appear or exist
Are empty of any essence,
And have only a conceptual or nominal identity.
Not the slightest distinction exists between the designation
And the nature of things that is symbolizes,
For there is a constant coemergence,
Which cannot be realized by external means.[132]

The same is true of all objects of our perception. Chocolate has no inherent taste independent of the taster. It does not have taste on its own side. Noise has no sound perceived within it. Without an auditory sensor, vibration is not transformed into sound. An odor is odorless unless perceived. Tree bark is neither smooth nor rough until some tactile perception occurs. Light without conscious perception is unknowable.

We can never experience the world beyond the boundaries of our own consciousness. Because we make sensory contact and label objects we come to believe that the perception of our senses is direct knowing. In fact, it is as though consciousness is immersed in the center of a crystal ball, believing reflections of the interior walls to be the exterior itself. Consciousness renders subject into object, and then forgetting the origin of its own creation, consciousness is either attracted to or repelled by its own emanations.

The mind is an organizer of fields of consciousness, a perceiver of reflected forms interpreted in consciousness. The attributes of the forms we perceive are always conjunctively an aspect of our sensory apparatus and consciousness.

Man as assembler of the field of consciousness within which he lives, mistakenly views his perceptions as being in one to one accordance with some tangible reality. However, if all the objects he views are absent of the self nature he imposes upon them, then logically, his own self nature is also not evident.

Considered from another perspective, if all that you view has no knowable existence in its own right, then you as the perceiver cannot stand alone as a verifiable entity. That it not to say that you do not exist in the conventional sense, rather in the absolute sense, consciousness configures within a field of ignorance.

Adi Da, in his monumental spiritual masterpiece, "The Dawn Horse Testament", illuminates *Divine Ignorance*.

> *You (As the conditional self, or body-mind-self) Can (and Do) experience and know (Whether Directly Or Indirectly) All Kinds Of Details (Whether True Or False) About things, others, or conditional events, but You (As the conditional self, or body-mind-self) Do Not and Cannot Ever (In Fact or In Reality) experience or know What any thing, other, or conditional event, and Observe That This Is So. Consider The Letter "M", For Example. Picture It In mind, or In print, or Write It Down By hand, Even many times. Consider All That You (As the psycho-physical self) experience or know About the Letter "M". Do You (in mind or in body) experience or know What the Letter "M" Is? Is? Altogether and Really Is? No. And What Does This Consideration Reveal About You and As You (the Presumptuous body-mind-"I")? Indeed, What Is the body? What Is the mind? What Is "You"? Through Such Consideration, Feel and Be The Feeling Of This "Ignorance" Itself. That body-Transcending Feeling-Ignorance Is The Native Intuition Of What Is (and Of The Only One Who Is).*[133]

Adi Da reveals how everything conceptually designated is originated in non-binding modifications of consciousness:

> *No Matter what arises, You Are Consciousness Itself. You Are Never Really (or In Truth) Separately Identical To or Even Really (or In Truth) limited by what Is objective (or Objectified) To You, but You Tend To Feel or Presume Specific (or Separate) Identification With (or Else limitation by) objective (or Objectified) conditions, Until You Are Able To Inspect (and To Be Inherently, and Inherently Perfectly, Identified With) Your <u>Real</u> (or Native, or Inherent, and Inherently Perfect) "Situation", Which Is Always Already Free Consciousness Itself, The Inherently Free Subject (or Perfectly Subjective Being) In The (Apparent) Context Of conditional objects (or Of Apparently Objectified Light), and Who (It Must Be Realized) Is the Self-Existing, Self-Radiant*

Condition or Being or Person That Is Always Already Prior To all conditional objects and Always Already Prior To Apparently Objectified Light (or Apparently Objectified Spirit-Energy) Itself. Therefore, the points of view of body and mind (and their Perceptions, Conceptions, or Presumptions) Are Secondary To and Utterly Dependent Upon The "Point Of View" Of Consciousness Itself (and The Perception, Conception, or Presumptions Associated With Consciousness Itself). Indeed, the Perceptions, Conceptions, or Presumptions Based On the points of view of body and mind Could Not Even Be Made Were body and mind Not Founded In (or Witnessed By) Consciousness (and When the body-mind and the conditional worlds Are Finally Recognized To Be Merely Apparent and Un-Necessary and Non-Binding Modifications Of the Transcendental, Inherently Spiritual, and Necessarily Divine Self-Condition, Then There Is Only You, Only God, Only "Bright" Consciousness, Only Free Love-Bliss, Only The Perfectly Subjective Feeling Of Being Itself).[134]

Einstein once said that physics is ultimately the study of the mind. Adi Da is stating an even more encompassing consideration; that mind, body, perceptions, conceptions, all arise in consciousness. Consciousness is without priority, and when unmodulated by perception is *seen* to be the inherently spiritual Self. Consciousness, that had been perfectly clear or empty prior to the first thought or perception arising becomes momentarily occupied with the newly emergent thought. It is not attached, or permanently modified by the thought. It merely witnesses whatever arises. Every thought, perception, conception or presumption that you have ever had arose in consciousness, stayed awhile and left. You have never been truly bound to modifications in consciousness. The purpose of meditation is to discover the nature, characteristics, and identity of consciousness when not modulated by discursive mind. Consciousness not modulated by thought is radically sane, infinitely rich, paradoxically empty, and the path to spiritual awakening.

Examining The Mind

We live our lives in consciousness, flitting from one perception to the next. We believe that all of these perceptions are connected in time, and that a very real future, present and past exists. We consider what we did yesterday, what will happen to us tomorrow and what is happening now. Rarely do we consider that we may be deceiving ourselves, living in the midst of illusion, self-bound to our fallacious inner dialogue. So strongly are we tied to our illusions that quite often we will lie, even kill, commit suicide, or at the least become severely depressed in order to maintain our myths. It is often easier to see the myths of other people and cultures, and how people are bound to self-destructive patterns of living, but rarely is it possible to see our own deceptions.

As children we are inculcated via language to a family, societal, and worldview by parents, friends, teachers, and the media. For the most part we consume what we are told without question. We become egocentric, ethnocentric, religiocentric and nationalistic in our belief system. We arrive in this life, and without our consent acquire a complete set of tax and legal regulations. We adopt cultural and sexual mores, often with only surface examination. We complain about taxation but rarely exercise our right to vote. According to current surveys more than half of married couples do not honor their marriage vows; and yet, ironically we are a country of puritans, severely judging figures in public life that stray from the so-called norm. We give lip service to our notions of morality, while the media, cognizant of the divergence in what we say and where we spend, exploits female sexuality. Women spend more on cosmetics and clothing in order to be sexually attractive than the individual national budgets of more than half the nations on this planet. We ostensibly deny our erotic side through our professed standards of morality, while it is quite evident that we are preoccupied with sex. Our national preoccupation however, is not erotic, passionate, heart-felt loving, but rather as most often expressed on the soaps and in the movies by pubescent mentalities, merely emotionally stunted sexually motivated behavior.

Perhaps there is some connection between our lurid interests, and the fact that we are the most litigious, divorce-laden society in the history of mankind. We wonder why one person in ten requires food stamps; why we have more people per capita in prison than any other nation; why drug abuse is a national blight; why crime is rampant in our cities; why our school teachers are being battered by students and parents alike; why there are so many who are home-less; why "the good life" is fading from sight? As the twenty-first century advances it is becoming increasingly apparent that the dream of unlimited material possession, given birth and credence by the commercially driven technocracy called modern civilization, is leading us further towards ecological disaster and spiritual bankruptcy.

Just what is the good life? Countless competing philosophical and religious groups compete for our allegiance. How are modern men and women to find their way through this plethora of competing and often contradictory interests? It is my belief that if any group has priority of truth, then that truth should be self-evident. We must first learn how to establish truth for ourselves, before we can assist in turning the wheel towards Nirvana. Universal compassion and wisdom, by necessity begins within the individual. The reformation of the outer world begins with the transformation of the egoic-self into spiritual awareness. Clarity of vision and purpose are attained when delusion and neurotic projection are eliminated.

The conventional world is what it is; and with, or without neurotic projection, endless worry, or discursive elaboration, unfolds unceasingly. We do not ultimately know what is happening, who we are, or where we are going. We have gotten to this mystical point, by the forces of nature, the grace within, the manifestation of the spirit. We have never experienced somewhere where "nothing" exists. There is no place that either we, or the scientist, or anyone has ever found "nothing". Suchness seems to surround us totally. Likewise we have been told that we come into existence at birth, and die at the end of our physical existence. However, in our experience, no one has direct knowledge of their coming into being, nor has anyone ever revealed their experience of death or permanent annihilation of the spirit. Both birth and death are myths of our culture. Past present, future, birth, death are all concepts that only exist in thought. Mind creates and validates these concepts. To prove that these concepts of birth and death exist beyond mind, by utilizing discursive reasoning, is like a dog chasing its tail. When dualistic projections cease—consciousness just is; nothing is prior to consciousness; consciousness is without cause and transcends the three periods of time.

Gampopa – Mind's Manifestations

The great Tibetan sage Gampopa describes the stages in which the unfolding and understanding of three aspects of mind takes place. Through the continued practice of meditative absorption and mindfulness the meditator will witness and understand the three aspects defined:

> *The essence, nature, and characteristics of mind are the three aspects to be defined. The essence of mind consists of clarity and nondiscrimination. The nature of mind is [emptiness] detached from any absolute arising, dwelling, or dissolving, while its characteristics manifest themselves on the levels of both samsara and nirvana. The meditator will therefore realize the essence of mind at the one-pointed stage, the nature of mind at the nondiscriminatory stage, and the characteristics at the one flavor stage.* [135]

The Nature Of Time-Space and Sanity

The meditator who has stopped the world *sees* that time has neither duration nor existence. The present is that which is always perceived. Thoughts of past and future events are representations in consciousness occurring in the eternal *now*. We can never bring into this moment some perceived 'actual' past or anticipated future. The present is always slipping away. Thus, the three planes of phenomenal existence are the products of mind only.

To be truly awake in this life is to actualize creative divinity within the conventional sense of experience, but not to drown within the illusions of time-space. Within the ever-present moment we have the opportunity to laugh, to love; to toil with strength, knowledge and resurgence of the spirit. Without toil life would be an eternal satedness; and without challenge, experience, failure, or triumph. Triumph can never be experienced without the prior experience of failure, nor strength without the prior experience of weakness. Unconditional love lies beyond the contraction in consciousness of the egoic-self.

If we cannot grow beyond our childish dependence on others for self-reliance, and an external God for wish fulfillment, then we will continue to thwart our own growth. We must see beyond words to know that language is only a partial pointer towards experiencing the richness of life. We must transcend language to experience taste, feeling, smell, touch, and love. We must drop our ordinary state of discursive excursions into the theater of linguistic gymnastics, and surrender to the joyous feeling of exotic aromas, musical magic, artistic fantasies, and passionate living and loving. To strive to master the tyranny of the inner dialogue is to begin to be able to experience the flowering of the spirit. The flowering within leads to the mystical, non-verbal, unparalleled experience of divinity. Divinity is a word contrived by the masters of yesterday to point towards a knowing within the realm of man's ability. The word itself however, is only a pointer, and consciousness must be surrendered to infinity to experience, to feel, to know, the divine.

The search for sanity is not to be found within the teaching of the conventional world. The conventional world is ruled by words and the illusion of time. To find the meaning of life one must transcend words. To find the experience of passion, one must transcend words. To begin to put order into one own consciousness, one must transcend words. The self is ever beckoning with illusions of future success, past glories, and potential success. Why live hoping for potential success when you can surrender to this moment, and erase all knowing, judging and wishing? You can live in samadhi. Samadhi is the feeling of love-bliss.

Mastering consciousness begins with the practice of inner silence. The doorway to mental health, peace of mind, tranquility and understanding, is through silence. We all have great resistance to inner silence.

As you sit, book in hand, you are aware of the book, and your environment, and your presence. Your mind moves from one thought to another. You appear to be viewing your environment. More accurately, your environment and sense of *being* are arising in consciousness. Reflected light enters your eyes and is interpreted in consciousness as a representation of your environment. The view you are experiencing, right now, appears as though it is outside of yourself. In fact, you are witnessing a construction in consciousness, truly within the confines of your skull. Every color, every perspective, every shade is a multi-dimensional presentation within the confines of consciousness.

You encounter a stranger. He is young, poorly dressed, perhaps a foreigner. A little girl, holding his hand, looks up at him. She sees her father, a loving man, dressed in his Sunday finest. You see a poor man, the child sees her father. And if I am observing the three of you, perhaps I erect all of you in consciousness in some other manner! There is only apparent and illusory reality. We each receive visual representations in consciousness and construct reality from our own perspective. When we become attached to our judgments within the passing stream of consciousness, we fall asleep, as if in a dream, and lose our genuineness in the moment. Each and every one of us is a center of consciousness, with an individual worldview. It is not that the world beyond the boundaries of our consciousness does not exist in some mysterious way; it is that we continually forget that our internal dialogue upholds our unique point of view. When we smile, frown or judge, we believe the world has changed. The world is never truly existent on its own side—our attention is caught in illusion.

As witness to this mysterious world we become attached to self-created concepts within the passing stream of consciousness. When we sleep we experience all sorts of impossible changes in environment that are accepted as actually occurring. Walls mysteriously disappear, people suddenly vanish or appear, changes in locale are never questioned. As the witness to these events that occur in dreamtime consciousness, we often remain the unobserved observer. When we awaken from the dream and review the content we realize—it was only a dream. You believe that the difference between your nighttime dreams and daytime awareness is that dreams are not valid because they occur solely within your consciousness, and cannot be validated by anyone else. We forget, or never realize that the same is true of our daytime experience. I may sit next to you in a plane or train for hours, or work with you every day. The dream however, is still only yours. To awaken from both day and night time dreams is to be truly awake, sane, and alive.

When you become attached to a piece of the passing stream of consciousness you forget that, just as in the dream, you are never truly attached to that which you witness. When you relinquish your position in consciousness and wander in daydreams of neurotic reverie, you travel the labyrinths of mind. Your inner dialogue, for example, tells you that you were born and will die. No one has ever experienced their own coming into being. You take it for granted, because you see babies being born, that your coming into being was coincident with being born. Although the birth of your particular consciousness is believed not to be an experience within your awareness, you assume that what you have seen and what you have been told is true.

The beginning of consciousness is nowhere evident. The absence of things, or *nothing* is also nowhere evident, nor is there some place in time or space where *nothing* is existent. Everywhere we look, there is something, or existence. No one has ever reported, or witnessed a time, or place, of nothingness or void. A place, or time of no being is a myth of our age and culture. If no-being is a myth, then all must be derived from being, or that which is the underlying ground of All. Since being arises in consciousness, as well as the conception of the three periods of time (past, present and future), it becomes apparent then that consciousness, or being, transcends the three periods of time, as well as beginning or ending.

No one has ever experienced or reported their absolute non-being. We see that the physical body is no longer animated at death, and we assume that consciousness has ended. We have invented this ending of consciousness. A consciousness presently existing requires either an infinite number of previous beings and births to be existent, or consciousness has spontaneously arisen from nothing. For consciousness to have arisen from 'nothing' is implausible, since 'nothing' has never been observed. In fact, the paradox of 'nothing' is that for it to be observed means that it *is* something. For a past or future to be existent they must also be observable. Neither past nor future is observable. A Nagarjuna might observe that nothing and something, being and non-being, past and future—are neither existent nor non-existent, arising in consciousness in union with appearance and emptiness. When all of these words and mind games are surrendered in meditative absorption, it can be *seen* that there is no priority to consciousness. Consciousness is the utmost subject of subjectivity, transcends the illusion of the three periods of time, is without causation, and is omnipresent.

Just as the nature of our entry into this plane of awareness is a mystery, so is our apparent departure from this plane of awareness equally mysterious. In fact, if you meditate upon the coming into being of the perception of your present moment of experience, you will see that your present perception came into existence equally as mysterious as that of your very own life's coming into being. And the departure of that particular moment of experience just contemplated, left just as mysteriously as all prior moments of experience.

Dreams and perceptions drift across the sky of mind, creating the illusion of time upon the eternal *Now*. This apparent moment expires, expires, expires. We conceptualize the past and the future as though they are truly graspable occurrences. We may say I was once five years old, or last Thursday I visited my aunt. However, we can never truly bring the past into the experience of the present moment. We are always in <u>this</u> moment, and there never truly is a past that can usurp the present moment and exist in its own right—right now! We confuse remembering past events with there truly being a past. This apparent moment of perception is continually changing. Whatever drifts out of experience in this moment we label as past, because we have no other way of describing or dealing with it. Consciousness itself never changes, and is the unchanged backdrop upon which the perception of self and world arise. The objects of awareness continually paint the sky of consciousness, however the witness of this unfolding panorama is itself never changed. If the witness were to change there could be no personal sense of continuity or apparently perceived self—because in each and every moment of now there would have to be a new witness. If the witness of consciousness had solidity, form, shape, or color then this consciousness would only be reflective of its already given structural form, shape, or color. Let us search for and examine the nature of mind.

Search For The Mind

The Ratnakuta says:

> Search for the mind should be conducted thus: What is a lustful mind, a hateful mind, or an ignorant mind? Has the mind emerged in the past, does it do so in the present, or will it do so in the future? Very well, you

should contemplate the fact that the past mind has ceased to exist, that the future mind has yet to arise, and the present mind does not endure. O, Osung (Kasyapa), the mind cannot be perceived as dwelling inside, outside, or even in between. O, Osung, concerning the nature of mind, there is nothing to investigate, nothing to demonstrate, nothing to support, nothing to make it appear, and nothing of visible form.[136]

The second Bhavanakrama quotes the Ratnakuta:

[Buddha:] O Kasyapa, the mind cannot be found through a complete search. What is impossible to find is inconceivable. What is inconceivable is neither past, future, nor the emerging present. What is neither past, present, nor future is empty of essence. What is empty of any essence does not have any origin. What has no source of emergence has no cessation.[137]

There is no time in our existence that is not in this moment. The panorama of life continually grabs our awareness, but the witness-consciousness of this apparently changing moment is never changed. The witness-consciousness is that aspect of consciousness that is the unseen, unchanged observer of constructions in consciousness. The witness-consciousness notices, but is not bound to the perceived changes in consciousness. Once consciousness perceives its own witness in consciousness, a weird crossroad is reached. The witness-consciousness, the *double*, is *seen* to be dreaming the self. The sorcerer's self-construction collapses as the double, or witness-consciousness *sees* that personal history is an illusion constructed in consciousness.

Gampopa describes the intrinsic nature of awareness.

The essence of mind consists of three aspects: essence, nature, and characteristics. Its essence consists of the state of clarity and non-conception; its nature is devoid of any substantive mode of arising, dwelling or ceasing; and its characteristics refer to the dualistic appearance of cyclic appearance and permanent peace [samsara and nirvana].[138]

Having moved the assemblage point to the witness-position in consciousness the sense of time, space, and history can be *seen* to be illusions in consciousness. To transcend these illusions one must stop the world. Once the warrior has gained sufficient power to stop the world, the warrior *sees* that he does not have to return to the world he left, for he had never really been anywhere. The warrior seer can now expand the world through personal power, selecting the items of his world to construct a path with heart. While he still must deal with the destructive forces of nature, and his fellow man, he upholds his world through will rather than reason, feeling rather than talk.

Perceptions in consciousness are born anew in each and every apparent moment of time and space. The illusions of past and present and future are constructed within consciousness. If there were no consciousness how could time, space, or matter be conceived? By whom, and for what purpose? By what standard of measurement or experience would matter exist? If consciousness did not exist, then how could it be determined that matter exists? Ultimately, matter and the cosmos arises within consciousness. Nothing is prior to consciousness. Consciousness, or self-radiant being, has no prior cause and is the fundamental nature of the universe.

Jigmed Lingpa – The Nature Of Mind

Jigmed Lingpa summarizes the nature of mind from the viewpoint of Dzogpa Chenpo:

> As its essence is emptiness, it is free from the extreme of eternalism.
> As its nature is clarity, it is free from the aspect of nihilism.
> As its compassion is ceaseless, it is the basis of various manifestations.
> These are divided as three but in meaning they are indivisible.
> May I realize the state of the basis of Dzogpa Chenpo.[139]

In the Mahamudra tradition Je Gampopa describes how the undistracted state of ordinary mind is experienced:

> Whether one is absorbed in a nondiscriminating state, neither
>   affirming nor rejecting anything,
> Or cognizing diverse thoughts,
> If one is able to maintain a tranquil mind,
> Unmodulated by dualistic discrimination,
> And if one realizes the inner sense that this state is non-
>   discriminating awareness,
> One has discovered the essence of mind,
> Its inmost disposition, and mode of abiding nature.
> When such an understanding is dawning,
> One need not make efforts in meditation.

It will come automatically to him
So that he can neither stop nor abandon it.
Similarly, as diverse thoughts arise
Without his being able to obstruct them,
So does nondual awareness arise in the same manner.[140]

The unenlightened wander in the labyrinths of mind, endlessly reviewing past actions and anticipating future gain. By stabilizing the mind in tranquil absorption, and studying the abiding nature of mind while reposing in meditative absorption, we can begin to reclaim our sanity. If we are unable to achieve tranquil absorption through meditative practice, experiential insight into the nature of reality will not be possible. Application of intellect, teachers, gurus, books such as this, will lead only so far. The way to sanity can best be achieved and secured through mastering tranquil equipoise. Without mastering tranquil equipoise we live within the reflections of mind, wandering from one thought to the next, anticipating ultimate satisfaction and happiness in a future that never quite arrives. We must learn how to be at-onement with the moment by raising the banner of mindfulness.

The Sutralamkara defines tranquility and insight:

Having settled in its intrinsic state,
The mind first concentrates on itself
And then properly differentiates all perceptive realities.
These are tranquility and insight respectively.[141]

The Essence Of Mind

The essence of consciousness, the screen upon which the play in consciousness appears, is devoid of any substance or concreteness. If the essence were concrete, or the essence within which this moment is constructed froze like striations in marble, then the essence would have to somehow or other dissolve in order to allow a new moment to appear. We experience apparent successive moments of now, and our minds wander off in memories of yesterday, and considerations of tomorrow. We talk of a past that we can never experience in a moment of now, or any other moment of experience. Each apparent moment slips by never to return again. The images upon the eternal now slip and slide from awareness like the grains of sand flowing in an hourglass. The future is always not yet now. The present moment is sliding into eternity. Thus, the essence of awareness is space like, with image-like clouds of attention drifting in and out. The essence itself is clear, and when not clouded by discursive thought or imagery, bliss like. Each successive moment in time is simultaneously dissolving and appearing. The essence of consciousness is without beginning or end, transcends the three periods of time, and is beyond intellectual analysis. Your present awareness is <u>this</u> mystic moment, the transcendental, the divine. This very mystic moment can only be experienced by a consciousness willing to surrender the eternally moving discursive process. It is not that the conventional world ceases to exist, or that the mystic is now lost in time and space. It is that one comes to realize that the dream of discursive reasoning is only a small part of the experience of being, and that consciousness exploring its own nature is the doorway to sanity and growth. The Tsokcho Chenmo of Je Gampopa describes nondual awareness or ordinary mind:

> If at this moment one wishes to achieve liberation from the cycle of existence, one must recognize ordinary mind, for it is the root of all things. That which is designated as "ordinary mind" is one's own awareness. Left in its natural state, this awareness remains unstained by any [nonordinary] perceptive forms, unmuddled by dullness, depression, or thought. If one has discovered the identity of that mind one has discovered the self-cognizing awareness. If one fails to gain such an understanding, this ordinary mind remains with the coemergence of ignorance. However, the understanding of that mind is called awareness, the essence, the coemergent self-knowing, ordinary mind, unmodulated simplicity, nondiscrimination, and luminous clarity.[142]

The Characteristics Of Mind

The characteristics of mind manifest in diverse dualistic perceptions, described as samsara and nirvana. Due to the force of socialization, and especially the acquisition of language, inner constructions are viewed as outer realities. For instance, as infants we have no concept of the days of the week. Once taught that there are seven days in a week, and their names, we begin to believe that this particular day has an inherent name, i.e. *Monday*. If only *Monday* could speak, it would know 'itself' as *Monday!* We learn about time, and come to believe, for example, that right now, at this very moment, it is truly *eleven o'clock*. How it happens that it is simultaneously *four o'clock* in London, usually does not remind us of the relative nature of time. We come to believe that time and the names of things are the things themselves. We almost never question that minutes, seconds, hours, the months and days of the week are contrivances of man and have no self-existence on their own side, nor for that matter a side of their own. If we could accurately determine the so-called beginning of the universe we could change this year's designation to a more accurate one. Perhaps a year configured in the billions would appear on our calendars, checks, and deeds, — that is if a beginning could truly and verifiably be established.

We are taught the names of cities, and mistakenly believe that the name designates an objective reality. What, for instance, is Paris? Is it buildings? Perhaps people? Is Paris defined merely by boundaries? We are taught to identify thousands of exterior and interior manifestations and associate precise names with very imprecise characteristics. Out of the mysterious mentations of consciousness we fabricate and label reality. We continually refresh our illusory place in apparent space and time through the incessant inner dialog, and forget that we are the authors of our self-imposed reality. We wander within the labyrinths of night-time and day-time dreams, forgetting that we are the Creator of all that we project and label through the inner dialog. Subject and object are separated within consciousness as though we are actually witnessing a veridical split in interior and exterior reality. Comprehending that the world occurs within ones own consciousness, and understanding all phenomena to be devoid of intrinsic reality, is to become acquainted with transcendental wisdom. In the Flower Ornament Scripture, the heavenly enlightening being, appropriately named "Good Wisdom", comments on true seeing:

> *No view is called seeing,*
> *The birthless is called beings;*
> *Whether views or beings,*
> *Knowing they've no substantial nature,*
> *The seer dismisses entirely*
> *The subject and object of seeing;*

Not destroying reality,
This person knows the Buddha.[143]

When we are only aware of socialized dualisms, we become infatuated with the acquisition of material possessions and are tied to our lifelong pursuit of wealth and happiness. No matter how much we acquire, we want more. No matter how magnificent our achievements or acquisitions, others seem more desirable. Ultimate happiness is always just out of arm's reach. Happiness can never be derived through acquisition. Paradoxically, happiness is experienced when there are no wants! Happiness can never be objectified by possessions or status. Happiness is an achievement in consciousness. Happiness is the release of all tensions, desires, and knowledge. Happiness is simply the transcendence of ego in self-radiant being. Adi Da, advises that standing free of discursive mind, in the nondual feeling of being or *Love-Bliss-Feeling of Being,* is happiness itself:

If The Transcendental (and Inherently Spiritual) Divine (or Perfectly Subjective) Self, In The Apparent Context Of Manifest conditional Existence As a Separate individual self, or body-mind, Is To Realize Its Own or Inherent Happiness (or The Inherent Spiritual Condition That Is Love-Bliss Itself), It Must Stand Free As Itself (and, Ultimately, It Must Realize That mind, body, and their relations Are Itself). To Stand Free (As Consciousness Itself, Realized As The Native Love-Bliss-Feeling Of Being, Itself) Is the Characteristic Of Existence In The Context Of Both The Sixth Stage Of Life In The Way Of The Heart and The Seventh Stage Of Life In The Way Of The Heart (Although The Ultimate, and Inherently Non-Dualistic, Disposition Of Free-Standing Consciousness, Divinely Recognizing, and Inherently Transcending, all Apparent arising conditions, or All Duality, or All "Difference", Is The Characteristic Only Of The Seventh Stage Of Life In The Way Of The Heart).[144]

When consciousness is occluded by transitory defilement, the intrinsic luminous clarity and essence of consciousness is obscured by dualistic perceptions. In order to penetrate the dualistic obscurations, the meditator thoroughly examines the mind while remaining in a state of tranquility and mental equipoise. The meditator utilizes tranquil absorption to examine the mind itself. His examination reveals:

1.   The nature of mind reveals no original causality, and

it is devoid of basis or support.

2. The mind is like space. It has no form, shape, or color.

3. Although thoughts have no discernible source of emergence or destination they nevertheless ceaselessly emerge.

The Mahamudra states:

By thus examining the mind the significance of the nonarising [emptiness] of the mind through discerning wisdom, the meditator should examine thoroughly its fundamental root or intrinsic nature — the way someone analyzes a bone by crushing it with a stone — until he discovers the depth of the mind. By so examining the meditator will experience the mind's abiding nature, which transcends thought or expression, and will finally achieve the extinction of the discerning intellect and the dawning of nondual awareness.[145] Saraha comments:

> *The nature of mind, like space, is pure from the beginning.*
> *As one gazes at it, the act of seeing as such ceases.*

And again Saraha says:

> *The mind may be described through the analogy of the mind itself.*
> *When dualistic thoughts are cleared*
> *The mind becomes stable and immobile.*
> *Like salt dissolves in water,*
> *So the mind dissolves itself in its intrinsic nature.[146]*

Adi Da – The Nature Of Consciousness

Adi Da defines consciousness:

Consciousness (Which Is That To Which and In Which conditional worlds, forms thoughts, beings, and self Are arising As Apparent Modifications Of Objectified Light, or God) Is Light, or God Itself.
Consciousness Is The Subjective Nature Of Light, Energy, or God.
Consciousness Is The Subjective Nature Of The Cosmic Mandala and all conditional worlds, forms, thoughts, and beings, including one's own self.
Consciousness Is Self-Radiant Bliss, Happiness, or Unqualified Being.
Consciousness Is That In Which or As Which any being Always Already Stands.

Therefore, To Identify With Consciousness Is Also To Realize Freedom, Eternal Being, Bliss, Happiness, and Love (or The Self-Radiant Nature Of Light, Energy, or God).

Whatever arises conditionally or objectively Is Only An Apparent, Temporary, and Illusory Modification Of Light, Energy, Bliss, Love, or God.

11. REALIZATION OF THE FOUR YOGAS

The Heart Of Consciousness

Once we have seriously undertaken the mastery of awareness, there are various paths that could be explored in each mystic tradition. Although the language and cultural context within all traditions appears singularly unique, the resultant change in consciousness orientation is similar. I believe it is more useful, indeed imperative, for mankind to emphasize the similarities, rather than maintain the ethnic, cultural or religious differences of individual paths. All paths throughout recorded history have fostered spiritual heroes. However, mankind has never successfully linked the enlightened masters of esoteric traditions to provide ecumenical leadership. If, after all, the mastery of consciousness or enlightenment leads to true spiritual awakening beyond the traditional egoic stages of growth, then why not foster ecumenical enlightenment? As we begin the twenty-first century the failure of Eastern and Western systems of science, religion, and government to ennoble mankind and begin the journey towards paradise on earth has become all too obvious. What is the use of a smattering of enlightened masters throughout many of our spiritual traditions, if these masters do not become more widely acknowledged teachers. If mankind is to prosper, the masters of enlightenment must grow beyond narrow, cult-like organization, and operate within all fields of human endeavor; especially education, ecology, science, business, medicine, and government. It is within the realm of your possibility to become an enlightened being.

The four yogas of the Mahamudra, the teachings of don Juan, and the God realization of Adi Da, utilize dissimilar language to foster transcendental growth beyond the traditional stages of adult development.

This passage from The Lankavatara-sutra points towards the understanding of the four yogas of the Mahamudra:

Mahamati: O Illuminated Conqueror, all bodhisattvas and mahasattvas who possess the four dharmas will attain to the yoga of the great perfection. What are the four dharmas [yoga stages]?

[Buddha:] They are (1) meditation on the lucidity of one's mind, (2) abandonment of the view of [absolute] arising, dwelling, or dissolving, (3) understanding that external reality is without substance, and (4) a deep yearning for discerning awareness. O Mahamati, all bodhisattvas and mahasattvas who command these four dharmas will attain the great stage of yoga.[147]

Ultimately, in all systems of meditation, discursive reasoning and conceptualizations are stains upon the mastery of awareness. The purpose of meditation is to maintain undistracted mindfulness while aware of the nondual nature of consciousness. The nature of consciousness, or the abiding nature of mind, is clarity, emptiness and bliss. The abiding nature of mind transcends intellectual discrimination, and can only be realized through single-pointed focus of awareness. The abiding nature of mind is not an object in consciousness, cannot be intellectually examined, and transcends the intellect. The awareness of certainty regarding the mind's intrinsic nature will eventually be realized through sustained mindfulness.

The Lankavatara Sutra describes the discriminating-mind as the obfuscator of Universal-mind:

The discriminating-mind is a dancer and a magician with the objective world as his stage. Intuitive-mind is the wise jester who travels with the magician and reflects upon his emptiness and transiency. Universal-mind keeps the record and knows what must be and what may be. It is because of the activities of the discriminating-mind that error rises and an objective world evolves and the notion of an ego soul becomes established. If and when the discriminating-mind can be gotten rid of, the whole mind-system will cease to function and Universal-mind alone will remain. Getting rid of the discriminating-mind removes the cause of all error.[148]

The Chakgya Chenpo Yigeshipa mentions six ways of maintaining the unmodulated, natural state of mind:

Keep your mind in immutable simplicity, free from pressure or exertion, like a great eagle soaring through space. Settle the mind in stillness, like a tideless ocean! Maintain complete clarity, like the unclouded sun! Know that perceptions and feelings arise from the mind, like waves appear upon a river, and therefore settle the mind in its natural state. Let your mind be clear, unobscured, and without clinging, like a child gazing with wonderment at a temple. Maintain trackless consciousness, like a bird flying across the sky![149]

The realization of the four yogas of the Mahamudra, the third point of don Juan, and Adi Da's samadhis leading to the seventh stage realization, and culminating in Moksha-Bhava-Samadhi, will generally require considerable perseverance. Don Juan tells Carlos why rational men persistently hold on to unproductive modes of living:

> "For a rational man it's unthinkable that there should be an invisible point where perception is assembled," he went on. "And yet more unthinkable, that such a point is not in the brain, as he might vaguely expect if he were given to entertaining the thought of its existence." [150]

Don Juan's assemblage point is the equivalent of the witness-position of consciousness of Adi Da. He advises Carlos that sorcery and freedom of perception is not arrived at through incantation and hocus-pocus, but rather through making the assemblage point move to a new position. Carlos reminds Don Juan that this movement is not so easily acquired.

> "But you yourself told me that moving the assemblage point is so difficult that it is a true accomplishment," I protested.
> "It is," he assured me. "This is another of the sorcerers' contradictions: It's very difficult and yet it's the simplest thing in the world. I've told you already that a high fever could move the assemblage point. Hunger or fear or love or hate could do it; mysticism too, and also unbending intent, which is the preferred method of sorcerers." [151]

Don Juan describes unbending intent as the mindfulness required to maintain the assemblage point away from the customary position. Except in the most extraordinary of meditators, each stage of realization will be realized gradually—and only after considerable practice will absorption be with all-encompassing understanding and the ability to maintain the realization effortlessly. Persistence in mindfulness, studying the writings of meditation masters, and discussing stages not understood with teachers and fellow meditators will assist in simultaneous realization and perfection. The Lankavatara sutra states:

> The evil out-flowings that take place from recognizing an external world, which in truth is only a manifestation of mind, and from becoming attached to it, are gradually purified and not instantaneously. Good behavior can only come by the path of restraint and effort. It is like a potter making pots that is done gradually and with attention and

effort. It's like the mastery of comedy, dancing, singing, lute-playing, writing, and any other art; it must be acquired gradually and laboriously. Its reward will be a clearing insight into the emptiness and transiency of all things.[152]

Je Gampopa notes that it is important to understand the difference between thoughts arising in consciousness, and the unstained backdrop of unmodulated consciousness itself—*seen* by the meditator as luminous clarity, emptiness and bliss:

> *An inner sensation does not transcend the mind but arises within its realm. Like the sun's rays emerging through patches of clouds, the inner sensation of bliss, clarity, or nondiscrimination fluctuates, rising high one moment, falling low the next, or remaining steady. If the meditation on inner sensation is maintained without the mind becoming attached to it, mental defilement will clear by itself and understanding will emerge. Understanding consists of an unceasing stream of the mind's luminous clarity, without the duality of appearance and thought, meditator and meditation. This is described as simultaneous realization and perfection.*[153]

Consciousness is never truly attached to the objects of attention or mind. The mind or attention must be dissolved in its source—consciousness itself. The nature of consciousness is clarity, emptiness and bliss. When modulated by the objects of attention or mind, consciousness, the non-prior and absolute subject of subjectivity, is only apparently, not actually, split into subject and object. Consciousness, or the feeling of being, is the root of attention. Consciousness is the matrix in which the entire conditional cosmos of body, mind, and world appears. Consciousness stands prior to the cosmic mandala of world, body, mind, and attention. Adi Da in his Sixth Stage Of Life consideration advises the resubmission of attention into the source or Heart of consciousness: [154]

> *Even When the mind (as attention) Has "Fallen" Into The Heart (In The right Side), it will Tend To "Leap Out" Again. And If attention "Leaps Out" Of The Heart (or The Feeling Of Mere Being, Itself) it Immediately Identifies With thoughts, and bodily states, and every kind of psycho-physical condition of the self-Contracted (and Separate, and Everywhere Related) ego-"I". Therefore, In the Context Of the Sixth Stage Of Life In the Way Of The Heart, attention (and, Thus, the entire body-mind) Must Be Constantly Yielded At (and, Thus, Re-Submitted To) its By Grace Revealed Source (Which Is The Heart Itself, and Consciousness*

Itself, Felt As The Inherently Perfectly Feeling Of Mere Being, Itself), By Means Of The First and The Second Stages Of "The Perfect Practice." [155]

12. THE FIRST YOGA

Luminous Beings—don Juan

The One-Pointed Yoga—Mahamudra

Savikalpa Samadhi – Adi Da

In spite of, and perhaps because of the vicissitudes of life, progress varies with each and every individual. Don Juan considered a petty tyrant a necessity in order to challenge the aspirant to the limit. The yogic masters of the Mahamudra suggest elevating awareness to the meditative state when the mind is agitated in order to test the stability of meditation.[156] In a televised interview the Dalai Lama stated that evil occurrences may be used to strengthen our understanding and compassion. Adi Da has considered whether he might have had more seventh stage realizers if he had limited his teaching to a small select group.[157]

Because of the great ordeal of self-transcendence, the realization of each of the stages may fluctuate before stabilization is achieved. Stabilization is required for each of the stages before the next can be appropriated. Familiarity with meditative absorption will eventually bring about intellectual discernment. Intellectual discernment will lead to a direct experience of the yoga stage. Finally, direct experience will lead to the first yoga or one-pointed yoga, which is designated as a single pointed awareness of the mind's essential nature. The meditator will have gained insight into the simplicity of consciousness, which while manifesting itself uninterruptedly is detached from transitory thoughts. The direct experience to be ascertained is the awareness of certainty, beyond any doubt, that the abiding nature of mind is space-like and intrinsically empty. This nondual awareness is detached from conceptual modes of discrimination, and transcends the three periods of time. Tilopa comments:

A mind without directed focus is Mahamudra.[158]

Je Gampopa discusses the stains of clinging and attachment that obscure the great seal, Mahamudra:

The knowledge of the emptiness of duality may be free from attachment,
But it lacks the awareness of the mind's abiding nature.
Meditation not detached from duality
May bring the inner sensations,
Yet it lacks the awareness of the mind's abiding nature.
A view without realization may surpass all conceptual modes,
Yet it still remains the act of intellect.
A great mystic who has not eliminated his attachment
Will create the cause of his cyclic existence.
No matter how good his meditative absorption,
A dharma devotee who lacks compassion
Will drift toward the path of the hearers.[159]

Unenlightened mind divides itself into apparent inner and outer reality, and abides in illusory duality. The stain on the one-pointed stage is the meditator's clinging to inner sensations, or attachment to the perceived reality of dualism. The perfection of the one-pointed yoga is the detachment from the psychophysical aggregates and purification of the five sense consciousnesses. Mindfulness is focused on nondual awareness, the space-like essence that is detached from any of mind's manifestation. Tashi Namgyal illuminates the perfect view:

In short, the meditator has perfectly determined the abiding nature of
internal and external realities when he experiences the dawning of the
determinate awareness of it coupled with an illusion-like sensation,
perceiving every thought as being the union of clarity and emptiness
and every appearance as the union of appearance and emptiness.[160]

The unobstructed inner avenue of emptiness gives rise to unceasing appearance. The mind's abiding nature can neither be lost nor attained. The meditator will cognize appearance and emptiness in the intrinsic unity of nondual awareness. Je Gampopa emphasizes that whether delusion is absent or present, the abiding nature of mind is not modified:

When the mind is distracted, delusion emerges;
When mindfulness is present,
The mind's essential state emerges.
This is indeed deluded duality.
Such alternation of abatement and attainment
Escapes my comprehension.
If such duality were inherent in meditation,

Both acceptance and abandonment would be worthwhile
And to eliminate them would be fallacious.[161]

After settling the mind repeatedly, an awareness of certainty will dawn regarding the abiding nature of mind. Settling the mind while relaxing and repeatedly dissolving perceived dualities will reveal the existential ground of clarity and emptiness. Je Gampopa verifies the space-like, immutable essence of mind:

Attainment through mindfulness and delusion through distraction
Are the creations of mind.
In reality neither attainment nor distraction exist.[162]

Unenlightened mind believes itself to be viewing the world detached from its own manifestation. Enlightened mind realizes that it *is* this nondual, apparent plane of existence (appearance in union with emptiness), rather than the unenlightened mind's perception of viewing a separate phenomenal world apart from the manifestation of its own awareness.

Don Juan – Luminous Being

In Tales of Power, don Juan relates to the first and second yogas through a consideration of man as a luminous being:

"I'm saying that we all are unfathomable beings, luminous and boundless. You, Genaro and I are stuck together by a purpose that is not our decision. Today I have to pound the nail that Genaro put in, the fact we are luminous beings. We are perceivers. We are boundless. The world of objects and solidity is a way of making our passage on earth convenient. It is only a description that was created to help us. We, or rather our reason, forget that the description is only a description and thus we entrap the totality of ourselves in a vicious circle from which we rarely emerge in our lifetime." [163]

Don Juan realizes the essence of mind to be luminous and boundless. He *sees* that the world of objects and solidity is only a description, without inherent validity on its own side. He admonishes Carlos that we become snared in self-made descriptions through *reason;* and entrap the totality of ourselves, our luminous, boundless essence of awareness, in discursive reasoning. Our totality is the union of appearance and emptiness in nondual awareness.

While don Juan utilizes the metaphor of luminous beings for the first yoga, he describes *self-importance as the force which keeps the assemblage point fixed where it is at present.*

> *He continued his explanation, saying that sorcerers are absolutely convinced that by moving our assemblage points away from their customary position we achieve a state of being which could only be called ruthlessness. Sorcerers knew, by means of their practical actions, that as soon as their assemblage points move, their self-importance crumbles. Without the customary position of their assemblage points, their self-image can no longer be sustained. And without the heavy focus on that self-image, they lose their self-compassion, and with it their self-importance. Sorcerers are right, therefore, in saying that self-importance is merely self-pity in disguise.[164]*

> *"For a sorcerer, ruthlessness is not cruelty. Ruthlessness is the opposite of self-pity or self-importance. Ruthlessness is sobriety."[165]*

For don Juan, ruthlessness or sobriety comes about with the dissolution of our self-importance. Moving the assemblage point is the cornerstone of erasing self-pity, and self-compassion. Moving the assemblage point to the place of sobriety, or luminous boundless awareness, enables the meditator to *see* the illusory nature of the self. Moving and stabilizing the assemblage point in luminous clarity is accomplished through mindfulness. Don Juan relates to Carlos how we get lost in the labyrinths of mind:

> *Don Juan said that human awareness was like an immense haunted house. The awareness of everyday life was like being sealed in one room of that immense house for life. We entered the room through one magical opening—birth. And we exited through another such magical opening—death.*

> *Sorcerers, however, were capable of finding still another opening and could leave that sealed room while still alive. A superb attainment, but their astounding accomplishment was that when they escaped from that sealed room they chose freedom. They chose to leave that immense, haunted house entirely instead of getting lost in other parts of it.[166]*

Mahamudra – The One-Pointed Yoga

The one-pointed yoga for the Mahamudra meditator is the focus of awareness on the mind's essential nature. The meditator has realized the essence of mind as being the union of luminous clarity and nonidentity. This essence is space-like, and detached from any thought while manifesting itself with clarity, emptiness, and bliss. The meditator is able to maintain this one-pointed mindfulness while blending arising thoughts with the essential nature of mind— clarity emptiness, and bliss.

Longchen Rabjam – Dzogpa Chenpo

Longchen Rabjam illuminates the one-pointed yoga from the Dzogpa Chenpo frame of reference:

> When the reflection of the moon appears in a pond, the water and the reflection of the moon are inseparable. Likewise, when things appear before the mind and when they are being apprehended by mind, the mind is inseparable from the appearances. It should be understood that the appearances before the mind are the apprehended phenomena and not the appearing objects. The object of appearances and its emptiness are inseparable like water and the reflection of the moon in water.[167]

Hua-Yen School – No Thought

In the first of five cessations, from the Hua-Yen school of Buddhism, the ancient seer, Fa-tsang, clarifies the no-thought of silent knowledge:

> If sentient beings can contemplate no thought, this is called entering the gate of true thusness.
> ...First is cessation of the pure emptiness of things and detachment from objects. This means that things in ultimate truth are empty and quiescent in their fundamental nature; things in conventional truth seem to exist yet are empty. The ultimate and conventional, purely empty, are null and groundless; once relating knowledge is stilled, objects related to are empty and open. At the moment of true realization, cause and effect are both transcended. The Vimalakirti scripture says, "The truth is not in the province of cause, nor in effect. Based on this doctrine we call it cessation by awareness of the pure emptiness of things and detachment from objects."[168]

Savikalpa Samadhi – Cosmic Consciousness

Savikalpa samadhi momentously heralds the arrival of spiritual awakening. The meditator's consciousness appears to implode upon itself, revealing the vastness of cosmic consciousness. Daniel Brown, in *Transformations of Consciousness,* discusses the first moment of enlightenment:

> The experience of the first moment, basis-enlightenment, is identical across traditions. From the perspective of observable events, all events, content and activity—everything—drops away. This is called "cessation." What remains? Vast awareness. From the perspective of the point of observation, as the events recede from awareness, the locus of awareness shifts; it "goes to the other shore" or "changes its lineage" (Visuddhimagga, 22:3-9). Prior to enlightenment, awareness is inextricably bound up with mental activity and events. The point of observation and observable event occur as if inseparable. When awareness shifts its locus during basis-enlightenment, the association between event and awareness is permanently severed.[169]

Usually, the meditator has initially only a brief glimpse of unitary consciousness, or satori. An effective method proposed by Hubert Benoit for stilling the mind, and revealing unitary consciousness, is the adoption of inward looking attentiveness, while remaining poised, and waiting for the response from ones inner self—to the inward posed directive—*Speak, I am listening.*

> It is easy for me to verify concretely that the active attention to my inner world is without object. If I take up, in face of my inner monologue, the attitude of an active auditor who authorizes this monologue to say whatever it wishes and however it wishes, if I take up the attitude which can be defined by the formula "Speak, I am listening", I observe that my monologue stops. It does not start up again until my attitude of expectation ceases.[170]

This nondual state of awareness may spontaneously unfold as the result of working with a Zen koan, or the method favored by the incomparable Ramana Maharshi, asking oneself repeatedly —*Who am I?*

> By inquiring into the nature of I, the I perishes. With it you and he [objects in consciousness] also perish. The resultant state, which shines as Absolute Being, is one's own natural state, the Self—The only inquiry leading to Self-realization is seeking the source of the "I" with in-turned mind and without uttering the word "I"—If one inquires "Who Am I?" within the mind, the individual "I" falls down abashed—and immediately Reality manifests itself spontaneously as "I-I" [absolute non-dual subjectivity, utterly without object].[171]

Mahamudra – Je Gayre

When the unitary consciousness is achieved Je Gayre advises:

> *Upon achieving the state of the one-pointed yoga*
> *One should dissolve all inner sensations*
> *And remain in that pure state*
> *Without any attempt at meditation.*[172]

Longchen Rabjam – Dzogpa Chenpo

Longchen Rabjam discusses the significance of the nonexistence of the apprehended egoic self:

> *By gaining experience in the significance of not finding the thought of attachment to "I" and "self" by investigation, one realizes the non-existence of the apprehended "self of person" and thereby (one realizes) the non-existence of the apprehender. One has already realized the non-existence of the "self phenomena", since the apprehended is non-existence in essence. After realizing the two emptinesses of self, both the objects among which one takes samsaric birth and the subject who takes birth. The liberation of samsara as the non-existent in true nature is the attainment of the vision of nirvana, because samsara is nothing else than mind—If one realizes thus, even if one could not attain liberation in this life, it is certain that one will do so in the next one—It is like "the karma of definite effect", by which, if one has committed a grave evil or a virtuous act, it is impossible that one will not experience its effects in the next life.*[173]

Don Juan – Losing The Human Form

For don Juan the death of the self, or losing the human form, represents the birth of the sorcerers struggle for assuredness:

> *"The sorcerers' struggle for assuredness is the most dramatic struggle there is," don Juan said. "It's painful and costly. Many, times it has actually cost sorcerers their lives."*
> *He explained that in order for any sorcerer to have complete certainty about his actions, or about his position in the world, or to be capable of utilizing intelligently his new continuity, he must invalidate the continuity of his old life. Only then can his actions have the necessary assuredness to fortify and balance the tenuousness and instability of his new continuity.*
> *"The sorcerer seers of modern times call this process of invalidation the ticket to impeccability, or the sorcerers' symbolic but final death," don*

Juan said. "And in that field in Sinaloa, I got my ticket to impeccability. I died there. The tenuousness of my new continuity cost me my life." [174]

Hua-Yen School – Voidness Of Person

In the second of five cessations, from the venerable Hua-Yen school of Buddhism, Fa-tsang elucidates the voidness of person:

Second is cessation by contemplation of the voidness of person and cutting off desire. That is, the five clusters have no master—this is called void. Empty quietude without any seeking is called cutting off desire. Therefore it is called cessation by contemplation of the voidness of person and desire. [175]

Adi Da – Ego Death

Adi Da discusses man's plight in living with the ego and without enlightenment:

There is no Enlightenment, no evolutionary entrance into the Spiritual Condition of human existence, without ego-death, or transcendence of the mind. There must be the literal death of the separate and separative consciousness. In this moment, you are holding on to your separative consciousness as if it were something tangible and material. You possess yourself through a great contraction of body and psyche. By virtue of this gesture, you have become rigid, mediocre, deluded, relatively loveless, self-possessed, and isolated. To be without inner consciousness is, for you, unthinkable. To be incapable of feeling yourself as a separate consciousness is, for you, a terrifying prospect. Nevertheless, that is precisely the realization with which you must become completely comfortable. [176]

It is only after ego-death, or the transcendence of the mind, that the highest stage of human existence begins, the stage in which the body dissolves or yields to Love and Light. In the Mahamudra tradition, dissolving the egoic-self in consciousness is jnana-rupakaya— the illusory form of awareness.

13. THE SECOND YOGA

SEEING —don Juan

Conditional Nirvikalpa Samadhi—Adi Da

Mahamudra – The Nondiscriminatory Yoga

The inner essence is the characteristic of mind to be realized at this stage. The meditator cognizes the essence of mind to be without construct, like space, and to be absolutely detached from appearance. He recognizes the uncomposed simplicity of mind that is free from any clinging to emptiness, or attachment to perception. The meditator realizes the selflessness of all appearances in nondual union with emptiness. Savari explains:

If the mind were real, all other phenomena would be real.
Since the mind is unreal, who can understand
That the real thing exists?
Neither the mind and the appearances
Nor the investigator can be found.
Being unreal they are unborn and unceasing
Throughout the three periods of time.
The intrinsic nature [of mind] is immutable, abiding great bliss.[177]

The Sutralamkara instructs:

By continually harmonizing
With the power of nondiscriminatory awareness,
Intelligent meditators destroy the dense forest of defilement,
In the same way that a powerful medicine eliminates poison.[178]

The Vairocanabhisambodhi gives further instruction on the nature of mind:

[Buddha Vajradhara:] O Master of the Secret Path, a seeker should strive hard for enlightenment and all-knowingness in terms of his own mind. Why? Because the mind in its intrinsic nature is completely pure. The mind cannot be conceived as existing inside, outside, or in between the body. O Master of the Secret Path, the mind has never been seen by all fully enlightened, supremely attained ones—nor will they ever see it. Being formless, the mind has no color such as blue, yellow, red, white, maroon, or crystal shade. The mind has no shape either short of long,

either round or square; it is neither light nor dark. It has no sexual identity such as female, male, or sexless.[179]

The difficulty for the meditator at this stage is stabilizing the newly found awareness with the understanding of the foregoing passages. Only with perfect tranquility and insight can the meditator realize the essence of mind. The essence of mind is not a phrase merely to be understood; rather it is a state of consciousness to be witnessed, studied in consciousness by consciousness, and finally mastered. The meditator stabilizes consciousness one-pointedly, and with discerning wisdom studies consciousness like a jeweler studying a diamond under a loupe. Perfect vision can be facilitated through association with advanced meditators or spiritual guides who have already perfectly realized the nondiscriminatory yoga. Studying meditation scriptures will aid in assimilating the non-discriminatory yoga and the spiritual meaning of life. The Mahamudra refers to the second yoga as the nondiscriminatory yoga:

The term "non-discrimination" refers to the abiding nature of mind, which, like space, is detached from any absolute arising, dwelling, or dissolving, from any conceptual determination such as eternalism and nihilism, or from inward and outward movements.[180]

The Mulamadhyamaka-karika states:

It is neither dissolving nor arising,
Neither nihilism nor eternity,
Neither going nor coming,
Neither separate nor same,
Completely detached from all conceptual determination,
It is the perfect quiescence.[181]

Je Gomchung reveals:

The stain on the nondiscriminatory stage is the non-determination of the inner essence.[182]

Don Juan – *Seeing* Of A Man Of Knowledge

For don Juan, a man of knowledge *sees*. A man of knowledge feels the world, which is upheld by his will. *Seeing* is don Juan's metaphor for witnessing the world through feeling, rather than the reasoning of the internal dialogue:

"I told you once that our lot as men is to learn, for good or bad," he said. "I have learned to see and I tell you that nothing really matters; now it is your turn; perhaps some day you will see and you will know then whether things matter or not. For me nothing matters, but perhaps for you everything will. You should know by now that a man of knowledge lives by acting, not by thinking about acting, nor by thinking about what he will think when he has finished acting. A man of knowledge chooses a path with heart and follows it; and then he looks and rejoices and laughs; and then he sees and knows. He knows that his life will be over altogether too soon; he knows that he, as well as everybody else, is not going anywhere; he knows because he sees, that nothing is more important than anything else. In other words, a man of knowledge has no honor, no dignity, no family, no name, no country, but only life to be lived, and under these circumstances his only tie to his fellow men is his controlled folly. Thus a man of knowledge endeavors, and sweats, and puffs, and if one looks at him he is just like any ordinary man, except that the folly of his life is under control. Nothing being more important than anything else, a man of knowledge chooses any act, and acts it out as if it matters to him. His controlled folly makes him say that what he does matters and makes him act as if it did, and yet he knows that it doesn't; so when he fulfills his acts he retreats in peace, and whether his acts were good or bad, or worked or didn't, is in no way part of his concern.[183]

Seeing is a shift in perception from the verbal mode of dualistic thinking, to the nondual intuitive feeling of being. When judgment ceases, projections are no longer causes for decision. The man of knowledge is free to choose a path with heart with a depth of feeling unhindered by rationalizations, guilt, and other self-inflicted deliberations. Learning the difference between choice and decision is enhanced through familiarity with *seeing*. Coming to a fork in the road requires a choice or decision, and unless one *sees*, nagging doubts cloud our vision. The man of knowledge waits until *feeling* reveals the choice leading to a path with heart. Often we make decisions based upon logic and inner dialog, as well as the expectations of others, —and in so doing, deny our intuitive inner *feeling* which tells us our decision is not appropriate. When we act out of *seeing*, our *feeling* is in accord with our choice, and there is never reconsideration. Decision, rather than choice, nearly always leads to second thoughts. Learning to *see* is learning to be in accord with our feeling. A man of knowledge *sees* the union of appearance and emptiness, and exercises controlled folly to find a path with heart. Knowing that nothing matters more than anything else, he chooses (*sees* or feels), a path with heart.

Don Juan tells Carlos that sorcerers change feelings into intent:

> *"Only sorcerers can turn their feelings into intent," he said. "Intent is the spirit, so it is the spirit which moves their assemblage points."*
> *"The misleading part of all of this," he went on, "is that I am saying that only sorcerers know about the spirit, that intent is the exclusive domain of sorcerers. This is not true at all, but it is the situation in the realm of practicality. The real condition is that sorcerers are more aware than the average man and strive to manipulate it, that's all. I've already told you, the connecting link with intent is the universal link shared by everything there is."* [184]

Ksemaraja – Kashmir Shaivism

In the Kashmir Shaivist tradition Ksemaraja stresses that it is a meditators attentiveness to the states of consciousness achieved that allows him to assimilate present stages, and progress to advanced states. For Ksemaraja the perfect practice results in the Supreme:

> *Speech cannot express, nor the eye see, the ears hear, or the nose smell, the tongue taste, the skin touch or the mind conceive that which is eternal. Free of all colour and flavour, endowed with all colour and flavours, it is beyond the senses and cannot be objectively perceived. O goddess, those yogis who attain it become immortal gods! By great practice and supreme dispassion[185]...one attains Siva, the supreme imperishable, eternal and unchanging reality.[186]*

Don Juan – Silent Knowledge

Don Juan explains how Carlos requires more energy than he can muster to enunciate and assimilate the side of silent knowledge, the older side of man that predates the modern era:

> *"It's a knowledge you cannot voice yet."*
> *"Why not?" I asked.*
>   *"Because in order to voice it, it is necessary for you to have and use an inordinate amount of energy," he replied.*
>   *"Silent knowledge is something that all of us have," he went on. "Something that has complete mastery, complete knowledge of*

everything. But it cannot think, therefore it cannot speak of what it knows."

"Sorcerers believe that when man became aware that he knew, he lost sight of what he knew. This silent knowledge, which you cannot describe, is, of course, intent—the spirit, the abstract. Man's error was to want to know it directly, the way he knew every day life. The more he wanted, the more ephemeral it became."

"But what does that mean in plain words, don Juan?" I asked.

"It means that man gave up silent knowledge for the world of reason," he replied. "The more he clings to the world of reason, the more ephemeral intent becomes." [187]

Hua-Yen School – Fa-tsang

In the third of five cessations, elaborated in the Hua-Yen school of Buddhism, Fa-tsang expounds upon the mystery of things established from a nonarising basis:

Third is cessation because of the spontaneity of the profusion of natural evolution. The arising of function based essence is called natural evolution; since evolution adapts to myriad differences, it is called profusion. Being constant, past and present, it is called spontaneous. This means that the elements of true thusness spontaneously follow conditions; myriad things arise together and spontaneously return to nature. Therefore we speak of cessation because of the profusion of natural evolution. Scripture says, "From a nonabiding basis all things are established." And that is what this means. [188]

Fa-tsang tells us that profusion is the characteristic of mind which manifests or evolves as samsara and nirvana. The three periods of time arise and return in thusness spontaneously. Cessation and profusion, emptiness and appearance, are established in the nonabiding basis, thusness or essence.

Adi Da – Conditional Nirvikalpa Samadhi

The second yoga, or samadhi, corresponds to Adi Da's witness-consciousness, and the meditators temporary identification with this stage, conditional nirvikalpa samadhi.

"The Witness-Consciousness Is Not A Result or Function Of the body-mind. The body-mind arises To It and In It, Like a face Reflected In a pond. Even So, The Reflection Is An Illusion (or An Appearance Only, and Even Only Temporary, and Un-Necessary). The body-mind (or the

self-Image that Is Apparently Reflected To You) Is Merely An Apparent Modification Of The Self-Lighted Pond (or Consciousness Itself)." [189]

The nondiscriminatory yoga or conditional nirvikalpa samadhi is conditional, in that its achievement requires the manipulation of attention in ascended states of awareness. Until there is a determination of the unity of appearance and emptiness or the witness-consciousness, the meditator will tend to cling to or seek the subtle bliss-like trance state of conditional nirvikalpa samadhi. The importance, however, lies in the meditators glimpse of the nondual essence of mind that is detached from all clinging and seeking, and is luminously clear and nondiscriminatory. Continued meditation will lead to identification with the witness-consciousness, and finally consciousness itself.

Adi Da – Witness-Consciousness

With continued practice the realization of Adi Da's witness-consciousness or conditional nirvikalpa samadhi, leads to resolution of the witness of consciousness in consciousness itself (sahaj samadhi):

> *Thus, Progressively, The Witnessing Consciousness Is Resolved In Consciousness Itself. The Life-Current, attention and the objects of attention All Become Resolved In (or Identified With) Consciousness Itself, through Contemplative Identification With Deep objectless Being, The Deep Well or Feeling Of Being Itself, Prior To all Motions or Modifications Of The Life-Current, and Prior To all acts of attention.* [190]

Adi Da cautions that the root feeling of relatedness is the first gesture in consciousness to become the separation from happiness. When we identify with the objects in consciousness feeling related through desire or clinging, the act of attention is shifted from the essence of awareness to its self-created objects:

> *The Root-feeling and "causal" <u>Stress</u> of relatedness is the Principal Distraction from Inherent Happiness, Because it Leads To all conditional "objects", "others", "forms", and "states", or all "things" (or all that is less than Happiness Itself).* [191]

Adi Da recognizes the freedom of the abiding nature of consciousness as the ground of the spiritual self:

When the Eternal Awakeness Is realized, the Spiritual and Transcendental Divine Self (or self-Radiant and Self-Existing Consciousness Itself) Spontaneously "Recognizes" all phenomenal conditions As Transparent (or merely apparent) and Non-binding modifications Of Itself.[192]

The Hevajra-tantra reveals the transparent, non-binding nature of consciousness:

The essence, form, and seer are unreal.
The sound and the listener are also unreal.
The beginning, middle and end are unreal;
So are samsara and nirvana! [193]

The nondiscriminatory yoga is an awareness of certainty of the nonarising emptiness of consciousness. The *Eternal Awakeness* of Adi Da is the Love-Bliss of Divine Ignorance. The importance herein lies in elimination of the mind's attachment to phenomenal conditions as having absolute existence or cessation. Je Phagdru explains:

Then the nondiscriminatory stage will dawn!
This the holy ones describe as the seeing of the minds essence.
Such an intrinsic state is but nondiscriminatory simplicity,
The expanse of all realities.
No matter how one distinguishes buddhas and sentient beings
From the standpoint of knowledge and ignorance,
In reality they all have one ultimate nature,
Which is nondiscriminatory simplicity.
It is detached from the modes of eternalism and nihilism
As well as from the view of absolute arising, dissolving, etc.
It transcends not only the worldly concern for acceptance and abandonment,
But also all conceptual determinations.
Such is the middle path! [194]

Stains On The Second Yoga

For the Mahamudra meditator the stain on the nondiscrimination stage is the nonrecognition of the inner essence. The abiding nature of mind is the union of appearance and emptiness. The meditator, having an awareness of certainty in regard to the inner essence of emptiness, becomes intellectually attached to emptiness and is ill at ease with appearance or relativity. For the Adi Da meditator, the attachment to the inherent love-bliss of consciousness is the stain on the witness-consciousness:

> *The Sixth Stage Error Is the Tendency To Hold On to The (Inherently Subjective) Position Of Consciousness As A Reality Inherently Separate (or Dissociated) From Objective Light (or The Universal Spirit-Energy) and all conditional objects (or all that Is Made Of That Apparently Objective Light or Spirit-Energy). It Is The Tendency To Hold On To The Inherent Love-Bliss Of Consciousness By Strategically Excluding All Awareness Of (or The Tendency To Grant or Allow attention To) conditional objects and states.* [195]

Perfection of the non-discriminatory yoga occurs when the meditator has realized apparent reality, with perfect insight, as the non-dual union of appearance and emptiness. There is neither attachment nor clinging in this clear, empty, bliss-like awareness. Spiritual qualities blossom as the meditator dissolves the root of experiencer, the egoic-self. The incomparable Tashi Namgyal, of the Takpo Kagyü order, clarifies the nature of enlightenment:

> *The meditator has sown the seed of the manifestation of enlightenment in himself when he knows how to establish an illusionlike cause during his postabsorption by engendering enlightened thought and solemnly expressing the resolve to fulfill the wishes of other sentient beings. On the other hand, he has failed to sow this seed of the manifestation of enlightenment if he has not brought about the interaction of magnanimous causes and conditions and if he has found it difficult to produce compassion, even though he has realized emptiness.* [196]

14. THE THIRD YOGA

The Double—don Juan

Jnana Samadhi—Adi Da

Mahamudra – Yoga Of One Flavor

The Mahamudra expresses the third stage as the yoga of one flavor. On the lower level of the yoga of one flavor the meditator will realize that good and bad, up and down, inside and out, all reside in consciousness. On the middle level of the yoga of one flavor the meditator will destroy the root of duality in consciousness as he realizes the one flavor of consciousness. On the great level of the yoga of one flavor the meditator will blend all opposite realities with the intrinsic emptiness of the abiding nature of consciousness.

Thus the term "one flavor" encompasses the blending of many opposite realities, such as appearance and nonappearance, into one single flavor. Je Phagdru explains:

All these diverse things—
Appearances and nonappearances,
Thoughts and emptiness,
Emptiness and nonemptiness—
Are of one flavor in emptiness.

Understanding and the absence of understanding are of one flavor;
The distinction between absorption and postabsorption
Is dissolved into one flavor;
Meditation and nonmeditation are pacified into one flavor;
Discrimination and nondiscrimination are of one flavor
In the expanse of reality.[197]

Jesus – Gospel of Thomas

From The Gospel of Thomas, Jesus illumines entering into the kingdom:

Jesus saw some babies nursing. He said to his disciples, "These nursing babies are like those who enter the kingdom."

They said to him, "Then shall we enter the kingdom as babies?"
Jesus said to them,
   "When you make the two into one,
   when you make the inner like the outer
       and the outer like the inner,
       and the upper like the lower,
   when you make male into female into a single one,
       so that the male will not be male
       and the female will not be female,
   When you make eyes replacing an eye,
       a hand replacing a hand,
       and an image replacing an image,
   then you will enter the kingdom." [198]

Don Juan – Dreaming

The third yoga, understanding that external reality is without substance, is reached only with great difficulty. Our rational, linguistic side of awareness, the tonal, through which we fabricate and maintain our idea of the world, "dazzles us with its cunning and forces us to obliterate the slightest inkling of the other part of the true pair, the nagual." [199]

To understand the tonal and the nagual don Juan has us consider our dreams. When we are dreaming everything seems real. It is only after we awaken that we reflect on the unreality of our remembrance. When the apprentice on the path of knowledge stores enough personal power and sobriety to have lucid dreams, he is then in a position to see that the dreams which arise in consciousness during sleep are no more real than the occurrences that arise in consciousness during the so called waking hours.

I told you that Genaro came to show you something, the mystery of luminous beings as dreamers. You wanted to know about the double. It begins in dreams. But then you asked, "What is the double?" And I said the double is the self. The self dreams the double. That should be simple, except that there in nothing simple about us. Perhaps the ordinary dreams of the self are simple, but that doesn't mean that the self is simple. Once it has learned to dream the double, the self arrives at this weird crossroad and a moment comes when one realizes that it is the double who dreams the self." [200]

Carlos is not quite clear in regard to the impact of this, and don

Juan continues,

"You could have realized that (it was not a vision or hallucination) with
infinite clarity if you had not gotten lost in your indulging, and you
could have known then that you yourself are a dream, that your double
is dreaming you, in the same fashion that you dreamed him last
night." [201]

Je Lingrepa – Mahamudra

Je Lingrepa comments on dreams as being an aspect of the teacher
within:

The rootless mind dreamed
A dream during the third part of the night;
This was the teacher who showed the identity of dream-appearance with
the mind.
Do you understand? [202]

The key to understanding who the teacher is, is to consider our
dreams. Regardless of the content of our dream, the dream characters, and appearances, arise within the unity of consciousness. However many people may appear in your dream, all of their voices arise
within your consciousness. You are the master puppeteer. You are
simultaneously the witness and the voice of all the characters of your
dream. While the dream is witnessed, unless you are lucid and
awake within the dream, the dream appears as real. Once awake you
realize the dream was an illusion, and that all of the characters and
situations arose in union with emptiness and appearance. Now
awake, all appearances and perceptions arise in the union of nondual appearance and emptiness. Do you understand? Takpo Tashi
Namgyal elucidates:

When the meditator perceives the clarity of the perceptive form with its
unidentifiable emptiness as being the inseparable, denuded union of
appearance and emptiness, or emptiness and appearance, he has gained
insight into the intrinsic coemergence of appearance. The analogy of a
dream illustrates well this experience. Whatever diverse forms a dreamer
dreams such as the material world, the outer container, sentient beings,
and the inner flavor, they are nothing more than the functions of the
dreamer's subconscious. So are the immediate appearances of dualistic
distortions, which arise out of the unobstructed vitality of the mind's
innate emptiness and continue to arise until the meditators common

collective karma is purified. From the moment of its emergence an
appearance is not different form the mind's intrinsic emptiness.[203]

Dzogpa Chenpo – Dakini Dream

Meditators often receive extremely powerful dreams of knowledge
from the inner teacher. One such dream occurred just prior to the
death of Khenpo Konchog Dronme, of Dodrup Chen monastery in
Tibet. He related the following dream to his disciples:

> *I had a dream (although his disciples were sure that he didn't sleep). A*
> *woman [dakini] told me: "Sokhe Chomo says: 'This present luminous*
> *absorption is the realization of emptiness. Because if this is not the*
> *emptiness, which is the nature of primordial knowledge, then the*
> *Primordial Wisdom of the Ultimate Sphere of final Buddhahood and the*
> *present luminous absorption will not be able to be established as*
> *indistinguishable. This present luminous absorption is the Precious*
> *Majestic Virtue. Because, if all the virtues of the result are not*
> *spontaneously in it without need of seeking, then the primordial wisdom*
> *of the Buddhas and present luminous absorption*[204] *will not be able to be*
> *established as un-differentiable.' I told the woman: 'Yes, that is a perfect*
> *understanding.' In any case, if one extends it further by meditating on it*
> *through the path of Unmodified Natural Contemplation and if one*
> *realizes the total perfection of the intrinsic awareness, then this*
> *luminous absorption becomes as the Five Primordial Wisdoms. The*
> *clarity and no-concept which has not arisen as either of the two*
> *obscurations is the Mirror-like Primordial Wisdom. The freedom from*
> *falling into partialities and dimensions is the Primordial Wisdom of*
> *Equanimity. Knowing all the phenomenal existents without confusion is*
> *the Discriminative Primordial Wisdom."* [205]

The revelations of a realized guru are especially profound, and
sometimes even more so when given just prior to death. Dream
revelation from a dakini is an especially auspicious sign as the
female dakinis are regarded in Tibetan Buddhism as the highest
manifestation[206] of enlightened protectors of the secret Supreme
Yoga. Buddhist mystics regard the highest yoga doctrine as being
protected from profanization and destruction by the dakinis.
Khenpo Dronme reveals in his dream that he is being told by the
dakini that his present luminous absorption is co-emergent with
emptiness and the Primordial Wisdom of Buddhahood. The dakini
tells Khenpo Dronme that the Precious Majestic Virtue is spontane-

ously present, and without the need for seeking in his luminous awareness. If this were not so, the dakini relates, the wisdom of the Buddha would not be co-emergently established with luminous awareness. This is another way of saying that the seed of the Primordial Wisdom of the Ultimate Sphere of Buddhahood is present from beginingless time and undifferentiated from emptiness. Khenpo Dronme concurs with the dakinis perfect realization. He further relates in his dream that continued meditation upon the essence of awareness reveals the luminous awareness as the Five Primordial Wisdoms.[207] The abiding nature of mind with clarity and no-concept is the Mirror-like Primordial Wisdom. The seed of Buddhahood within the empty, non-arisen abiding nature of mind[208] reveals the freedom from falling into discursiveness through the Primordial Wisdom of Equanimity. The nondual realization of emptiness and appearance on the path of non-cultivation[209] is the Discriminative Primordial Wisdom.

It is said that the great sage Saraha, the spiritual father of all of the great saints of India, transmitted the teachings to Nagarjuna. Nagarjuna and Saraha in turn transmitted the teachings, the illusory form of awareness, also known as the rainbow form, to Savari. According to the Kagyü Mahamudra tradition the nonmeditation stage is the union of the Supreme Illusory Form[210] and luminous awareness on the path of non-cultivation.

Savari describes the abiding nature of mind:

It is neither going nor standing still,
Neither static nor dynamic,
Neither substance nor nonsubstance,
Neither appearance nor emptiness,
The nature of all things, like space,
It is without any movement.
One may call it "space"
But is empty of any essence
And as such transcends definitions
Such as real or unreal,
Existent or nonexistent,
Or anything else.
Thus not the slightest distinction exists
Between space, the mind, and intrinsic reality.

Only their designations are different,
But they are unreal and false.[211]

What then is the difference between space and mind? Space is not self-cognizing awareness.

The meditator having quieted the mind, and sustaining awareness single-pointedly, is aware of the space-like essence of consciousness. When the focus of mind shifts the space-like essence vanishes. When the focus of mind is reestablished single-pointedly, it is seen that the essence is unstained by the senses or dualistic concepts, and transcends the three periods of time.

Hua-Yen School – Light Without Thought

In the fourth of five cessations, elaborated in the Hua-Yen school of Buddhism, Fa-tsang elucidates light without thought:[212]

Fourth is cessation by the light of concentration shining forth without thought. This refers to the precious jewel of the blessed universal monarch with a pure jewel net.[213] *That is to say, the essential nature of the jewel is penetratingly bright; the ten directions are equally illumined, as tasks are accomplished without thinking. Thoughts all acquiesce. Though manifesting extraordinary accomplishments, the mind is without cogitation. The Hua-Yen scripture says, "It is like a wheel-turning king who perfects the supreme seven treasures—their provenance cannot be found: the nature of action is also like this."* [214] *If there are sentient beings who enter the gate of great cessation and subtle observation, they accomplish works spontaneously, without thought, without cogitation, like that jewel equally illumining far and near, clearly manifesting, penetrating throughout space, not obstructed or covered by the dust and fog, mist and clouds of the two lesser vehicles [of individual salvation] and heretics. Therefore we call it cessation by the light of concentration shining forth without thought.*

Longchen Rabjam – Dzogpa Chenpo

Longchen Rabjam describes how enlightenment comes about:

The "basis" [in Dzogpa Chenpo] has three aspects: essence, nature, and compassion, which are the Primordial Wisdoms of the Ultimate body. It is the space-like Intrinsic Awareness, unstained by samsaric phenomena.[215]

It is also crucial to know the differences between the mind and Primordial Wisdom. Mind is a samsaric phenomena having stains of karma and its traces. Mind's objects are the delusory appearances of samsara, the sixfold objects.[216] When the true nature of mind, the Intrinsic Awareness, becomes free from mind, that is the attainment of enlightenment. Primordial Wisdom is the virtues of nirvana; it is free from samsaric karma, traces and concepts. The object of Primordial Wisdom is the space-like Ultimate Nature and Luminous Buddha-fields of Buddha-bodies, and Primordial Wisdoms.

Adi Da – Aham Sphurana

Adi Da elaborates on noticing the *aham sphurana, the love-bliss feeling of being:*

> *The "Aham Sphurana", or Consciousness associated with the Inherent Radiance of the Spirit-Current in the right side of the heart, is the First Sign of the penetration and transcendence of the "causal body", or "anandamyakosha" (the seat or heart of conditional bliss). The "causal body" is (apparently) conditionally associated with egoity (or separate Consciousness), in the form of an illusion that Consciousness is separate and unillumined in deep sleep. Truly, all illusions, being a part of mind, arise only with mind, and, therefore, only when dreams and thoughts arise in the dreaming and waking states.[217]*

Adi Da notes that the feeling of relatedness must be transcended in all states of consciousness, sleeping, as well as waking, until the essence of consciousness is realized. This essence of consciousness is not attached to the illusions in consciousness and is prior to all apparent modifications in consciousness:

> *When the self-contraction (in its root form, which is attention) is transcended in the Realization of Native or Inherent Identification with consciousness Itself (Prior to the body-mind), the Truth of Consciousness Itself becomes Inherently Obvious. And, thereafter, even if conditions apparently arise (whether in the waking, the dreaming, or the sleeping state), they are Inherently "Recognizable" as transparent, or merely apparent, and non-binding modifications of the Divine Self-Radiance of Self-Existing Consciousness Itself.[218]*

Adi Da – Jnana Samadhi

Adi Da reveals the ultimate identity of the witness of consciousness to be The Divine Person. The veiling of the knowing of The Divine

Person occurs because of identification in consciousness with phenomenal states of mind rather than the Self-Radiant Transcendental Divine Person. Jnana Samadhi (or Adi Da's sixth stage realization) is a state of ascended meditation that excludes phenomenal states by confining self-consciousness to itself. The corresponding stain of mind of the Mahamudra one flavor yoga is subtle clinging to substantive reality or emptiness. Becoming attached to emptiness impedes the meditator's practice and ease with relativity on the level of one flavor, or jnana samadhi. The point to be understood is that there is no priority to consciousness; it is attention that apparently moves from the well of being in consciousness and seeks the bliss of emptiness, or clings to appearance. In truth, attention is never truly attached to the apparent objects of perception or conception in consciousness. Adi Da explains the discipline of the first two stages of The Perfect Practice:

> The Discipline In the First Stage Of the Perfect Practice Is To Stand As The Witness-Consciousness. The Discipline In the Second Stage Of the Perfect Practice Is Deep Contemplation Of Consciousness and Deep Identification With Consciousness Itself.[219]

Stains On The Third Yoga

Adi Da observes the arising in consciousness of the apparent world, body-mind and apparent relations to the objects in consciousness as only apparent modifications of *The Universal Spirit-Energy*. Adi Da indicates that jnana-samadhi stage is stained when the *Witness-Consciousness* is not resolved in consciousness itself or the *Love-Bliss* feeling of being. For don Juan the stain on luminous being is the world of reason, or clinging to apparent modifications in consciousness; liberation occurs with enough energy to acquire and stabilize silent knowledge and the spirit of man. In the Mahamudra tradition Virupa declares:

> By detaching itself from the duality of observation and observer,
> The mind achieves self-liberation from division;
> By thus smashing the contrived practitioner
> The mind frees itself from striving and seeking;
> By discarding the concern for the fruit of inner development,
> The meditator unshackles himself from hope and fear;

By eliminating the sense of the "self" or the "I",
The mind emerges victorious in its battle against inner adversaries;
By dismantling the clinging to substance,
The meditator will gain liberation from both samsara and nirvana.[220]

The meditator at this stage of meditation may lose sight of the essence of mind through a lapse in mindfulness. However, once he succeeds in regaining mindfulness, he will again perceive the union of emptiness and appearance and the nondual nature of consciousness. He will liberate himself from the apparent arising of feelings and perceptions, and purify the source consciousness.

15. THE FOURTH YOGA

Total Awareness; The Third Point Of Reference—don Juan

Sahaj Samadhi; Moksha-Bhava-Samadhi—Adi Da

Mahamudra – The Nonmeditation Yoga

The fourth yoga, the yoga of nonmeditation is the transformation in consciousness into a fully awakened state. The Mahamudra describes three levels of attainment. On the lower level the meditator will recognize all appearances as a nondual unification of apparent external and internal realities within consciousness. Having realized the nonmeditation state he will no longer need to maintain this state with mindfulness, nor to seek absorption through meditation. This lower state will, however, have a very subtle clinging to the blissful sensations experienced during meditation. On the average level of attainment the meditator will be free of all clinging, and realize this state throughout the entire cycle of day and evening. A slight subtle consciousness will again, however, crystallize. On the great level of the yoga of nonmeditation the meditator will transform the subtle stain into transcending awareness, blending the luminous awareness attained through meditation with the awareness that has emerged spontaneously.

Mahamudra – The Nonmeditation Yoga

Gompopa illumines the perfection of Mahamudra:

> *Where there is no evaluation, any discriminating thought*
> *Will achieve a simultaneous arising and release;*
> *Where there is no deep attachment,*
> *Everything remains in even harmony.*
> *If one realizes this,*
> *The stream of meditation will not cease;*
> *One will become a sovereign*
> *Dominating the cycle of birth and death*
> *And will be free from any clinging to duality,*
> *Luminous awareness will prevail throughout the cycle of time.* [221]

Mahamudra – Enlightenment Of Dharmakaya

Mastery of the yoga of nonmeditation is an enlightened state that has cleared all stains of inner sensation and experience, and has achieved a harmonious blend of the understanding of the illuminating process with the abiding nature of the mind. Such a mind is completely detached from the duality of absorption and postabsorption, mindfulness and distraction. Je Phagdru states:

> By perfecting this nonmeditation stage
> The meditator attains naked, unsupported awareness.
> This nondiscriminatory awareness is the meditation!
> By transcending the duality of meditation and meditator,
> External and internal realities,
> The meditating awareness dissolves itself
> Into luminous clarity.
> Transcending the intellect,
> It is without the duality of equipoise and postequipoise.
> Such is the quintessence of mind.[222]

The Mahamudra illuminates the pinnacle of meditation, the nonmeditation yoga.

> The transcendent qualities of the nonmeditation yoga have blossomed in the meditator when he has achieved the rainbowlike physical transformation of his mortal body into the illusory form of awareness [jnana-rupakaya], when his mind has transformed itself into lucid awareness [dharmakaya], and when he perceives the countless buddha realms. No such transcendent qualities have blossomed in him if he continues to perceive his body and mind, the external worlds, and all sentient beings as impure and if he still has a slight mental clinging to his realization.[223]

Tashi Namgyal clarifies the spiritual goal of the enlightenment of dharmakaya:

> The meditator has completely germinated the seed of the transcending body when he has attained the enlightenment of dharmakaya, which consists of the inseparable union of infinite emptiness and his transcending awareness, and when he is able through inexhaustible cycles of his enlightened body, speech, and mind to give sentient beings the never ending spiritual benefits. If he still has to rely on his efforts to attain the cosmic realms of the buddhas, then the meditator has not germinated completely the seed of transcending body.[224]

The meditator having established the union of appearance and emptiness in nondual consciousness perceives the illusory nature of his particular body-mind. The illumined body-mind is revealed as rainbow-like and illusory, having the characteristics of appearance and emptiness. The apparent world arises lucidly in the essence of emptiness, without beginning or cessation. The countless buddha realms arise as the One plane of cosmic manifestation with each apparently separate manifestation in perfect nondual union of appearance and emptiness. With consummate courage the Buddha proclaims to the world the four states of fearlessness:

1) That he has attained the transcendental wisdom that directly perceives and penetrates into all diverse levels of knowledge.

2) That he has completely eliminated the mind's affliction and intellectual confusion.

3) That the joint development of wisdom and compassion is the surest way to liberation.

4) That inner delusion, lust, and hatred are obstacles to liberation.

The first two represent the supreme fulfillment of his personal aspiration, and the last two represent the fulfillment of his universal aspiration for the permanent good of all sentient beings.[225]

Don Juan – The Third Point Of Reference

For don Juan the quintessence of mind is realized as a third point of reference, *intent* or the spirit. He relates to Carlos that being in two places at once means the assemblage point has reached the place of silent knowledge:

He assured me that every nagual consistently did everything within his power to encourage the free movement of his apprentices' assemblage points. This all-out effort was cryptically called "reaching out for the third point."
"The third point of reference is freedom of perception; it is intent; *it is the spirit; the somersault of thought into the miraculous; the act of reaching beyond our boundaries and touching the inconceivable."* [226]

The shifting in orientation from the stream of consciousness to the witness of consciousness, and finally consciousness itself, is comparable to the sun finally shining through the obscuration of clouds. The sorcerer is simultaneously aware of the conventional world and ultimate meaning (the nondual union of appearance and emptiness). Moving the assemblage point is equivalent to being aware that it is attention that makes the world. A sorcerer, or meditator transcends the mind by dissolving dualistic attention in consciousness. Skilled in tranquil equipoise, the meditators experiential reality reveals the pause between ideas, the mirror-like clarity of unmodulated mind. This awareness of the innate simplicity reveals nondual, valid reality. The non-meditators worldly reality is conditioned by inner dialog and the senses, and it is perceived in a distorted way. For the Mahamudra meditator, unconditioned awareness, free of deluded duality is ordinary mind. Don Juan's third point, and the ordinary mind of the Mahamudra, is the connection between man and spirit:

> "What you're witnessing is the result of a lifelong struggle," he said. "What you see is a sorcerer who has finally learned to follow the designs of the spirit, but that's all."
>
> "I have described to you, in many ways, the different stages a warrior passes through along the path of knowledge," he went on. "In terms of his connection with intent, a warrior goes through four stages. The first is when he has a rusty, untrustworthy link with intent. The second is when he succeeds in cleaning it. The third is when he learns to manipulate it. And the fourth is when he learns to accept the designs of the abstract." [227]

Learning to accept the designs of the abstract represents the attainment of faith and spiritual awareness. Without spiritual awareness and faith in the designs of the abstract, awareness will be obscured by discursive elements. Having learned to accept the designs of the spirit, the meditator unites his meditative awareness with the spontaneously arisen luminous awareness and fulfills his personal and spiritual goals.

In *The Second Ring of Power* Gorda relates how don Juan clarified the concept of the mold of man. For don Juan the mold of man can be seen from the second attention or dreaming:

> He described the mold as being the source, the origin of man, since, without the mold to group together the force of life, there was no way for that force to assemble itself into the shape of man. [228]

Don Juan describes the universe as the play of the Eagle's

emanations, Gorda quotes don Juan as having revealed the nature of the mold of man:

> *The Nagual said that sometimes if we have enough personal power we can catch a glimpse of the mold even though we are not sorcerers; when that happens we say that we have seen God. He said that if we call it God it is the truth. The mold of man is God.*[229]

For don Juan, total awareness, or enlightenment, is an illumination that lights up the entire luminous egg:

> *Heightened awareness is nothing in comparison to the glow produced by a state of total awareness, which is seen as a burst of incandescence in the entire luminous egg. It is an explosion of light of such magnitude that the boundaries of the shell are diffused and the inside emanations extend themselves beyond anything imaginable.*

> *Seers who deliberately attain total awareness are a sight to behold. That is the moment when they burn from within. The fire from within consumes them. And in full awareness they fuse themselves to the emanations at large, and glide into eternity.*[230]

The total awareness of don Juan and the innate simplicity of the Mahamudra meditator's ordinary mind reveal the enlightened realm of awareness. The perfect vision of the nondual union of appearance and innate simplicity transcends the three periods of time and illuminates the entire luminous egg. For the Mahamudra meditator luminous awareness is in union with the supreme illusory form on the path of non-cultivation.[231]

Adi Da – Transcending The Cosmic Mandala

Freedom of perception and the clarity of ordinary mind represent the illusory form of being which is the union of earthly manifestation and spiritual being. For Adi Da, complete dissolution of the egoic self into total awareness reveals the source and identity of the luminous egg:

> *If the self-Contraction Is Directly (and Most Fundamentally) Understood, and If it Is Really (or Otherwise Effectively) Transcended In The Total Context Of The First Six Stages Of Life, Then the Total body-mind, all its conditional relations, and The Total Cosmic Mandala or Cosmos Of conditional Nature Are Utterly, Totally and Inherently Transcended In The Native Realization of The Always Already Free*

Transcendental, Inherently Spiritual, and (Necessarily) Divine Self. Just So, When The Self-Radiant (or Inherently Spiritual), Self-Existing (or Transcendental), and (Necessarily) Divine Self Is Realized, the Apparent conditional self (or body-mind), its conditional relations, and The Total Cosmos Of conditional Nature Are Inherently (and Divinely) Recognizable In The "Bright" Inherent Radiance (or Self-Radiant and Inherently Spiritual Love-Bliss) Of The Transcendental Divine (or Perfectly Subjective) Self. And Such Divine Recognition (or "Bright" Divine Samadhi) Ultimately outshines conditional Existence (or Translates Existence From the conditionally, and Only Apparently, Existing Cosmos Of conditional Nature To The self-Existing and Self-Radiant Divine Self-Domain).[232]

Hua-Yen Buddhism – Formless Cessation

In the last of five cessations, from the Hua-Yen school of Buddhism, Fa-tsang elucidates the formless cessation:

Fifth is the formless cessation in the mystic communion of noumenon and phenomena. This means that phenomena, which are illusory forms, and noumenon, the absence of intrinsic nature, mutually conceal and mutually reveal each other. Therefore it is called mystic communion. Moreover, because noumenon is revealed by way of practice, phenomena permeate noumenon; as practice arises from noumenon, noumenon permeates phenomena: they mutually affirm and mutually deny each other, so it is called mystic communion. Mystic communion means that great wisdom exists alone, its essence pervading the universe; great compassion saves beings by carrying out myriad practices. Compassion and wisdom merge; nature and characteristics both disappear. Therefore it is called formless cessation in the mystic communion of noumenon and phenomena.[233]

Flower Ornament Scripture

As told in The Flower Ornament Scripture - Buddha Flower Array, the World-Honored One "had arrived at the nondual ultimate perfection of Buddhahood and fully attained the equal liberation of the enlightened. He had realized the stage of impartiality of Buddhas, which is without extremes or middle, extending throughout the cosmos, equal to space." In a great assembly of enlightening beings is Universal Good, who after arising from a vast concentration called *the Buddha flower array*, delivers the pinnacle of enlightened discourse to the assembly. The following fragment metaphorically likens enlightenment to manifestations of co-dependently arising Nature:

> *Mental command is the level ground,*
> *Spiritual practices are the rivers,*
> *Pure knowledge the wellsprings,*
> *Sublime wisdom the forests,*
> *Emptiness the clear lakes,*
> *The branches of enlightenment lotus blossoms.*[234]

The Lankavatara Sutra – Noble Wisdom

The Lankavatara Sutra illuminates "the self-nature of Noble Wisdom, blissfully peaceful with the serenity of Perfect Love:"

> *Entering upon the eighth stage, with the "turning about" at the deepest seat of consciousness, the Bodhisattva will become conscious that he has received the second kind of Transcendental-body (Manomayakaya). The transition from mortal-body to Trancendental-body has nothing to do with mortal death, for the old body continues to function and the old mind serves the needs of the old body, but now it is free from the control of mortal mind. There has been as inconceivable transformation-death (acintya-parinama-cyuti) by which the false-imagination of his particularized individual personality has been transcended by a realization of his oneness with the universalized mind of Tathagatahood, from which realization there will be no recession. With that realization he finds himself amply endowed with all the Tathagata's powers, psychic faculties, and self-mastery, and, just as the good earth is the support of all beings in the world of desire (karmadhatu), so the Tathagatas become the support of all beings in the Transcendental World of No-form.*[235]

The Lankavatara Sutra – Perfect Love of Nirvana

The Lankavatara Sutra clarifies directly in terms of perfect realization the transcendence of the stages of meditation. Perfect realization is sustained by the abiding nature of the Buddhas, where luminous awareness comprised of infinite compassion abides in place of the no longer existent egoic self:

> *The Tathagata's Nirvana is where it is recognized that there is nothing but what is seen of the mind itself; it is where, recognizing the nature of the self-mind, one no longer cherishes the dualisms of discrimination; it is whether there is no more thirst nor grasping; it is where there is no*

more attachment to external things. Nirvana is where the thinking-mind with all its discriminations, attachments, aversions and egoism is forever put away; it is where logical measures, as they are seen to be inert, are no longer seized upon; it is where even the notion of truth is treated with indifference because of its causing bewilderment; it is where, getting rid of the four propositions, there is insight into the abode of Reality.

The Blessed One further clarifies the attainment and realization of the Perfect Love of Nirvana:

Nirvana is where the Bodhisattva stages are passed one after another; it is where the sustaining power of the Buddhas upholds the Bodhisattvas in the bliss of the Samadhis; it is where compassion for others transcends all thoughts of self; it is where the Tathagata stage is finally realized.

Nirvana is the realm of Dharmata-Buddha; it is where the manifestation of Noble Wisdom that is Buddhahood expresses itself in Perfect Love for all; it is where the manifestation of Perfect Love that is Tathagatahood expresses itself in Noble Wisdom for the enlightenment of all; —there, indeed, is Nirvana! [236]

The Lankavatara Sutra comments as to who will achieve the realization of Nirvana:

But no beings are left outside by the will of the Tathagatas; some day each and every one will be influenced by the wisdom and love of the Tathagatas of Transformation to lay up a stock of merit and ascend the stages. But, if they only realized it, they are already in the Tathagata's Nirvana for, in Noble Wisdom, all things are in Nirvana from the beginning. [237]

Shingta Chenpo – The Ultimate Body

Longchen Rabjam, the supremely enlightened author of Shingta Chenpo, clarifies the nature of Buddhahood that consists of the Buddha-bodies as the basis and the Primordial Wisdoms as the essence. The term *body* is to be understood in the sense of an aspect of the essence of consciousness, rather than as a physical body. Although the Buddha-bodies and Primordial Wisdom are elaborated for clarification, in actuality the meaning of the virtues and classifications are one in essence. The meditator actualizes the nondual unity of the Buddha-bodies as the basis of luminous awareness, once the dualistic self-contractions of the egoic mind are transcended. The meditator's accomplishment of the *Ultimate Body* has three aspects: The Buddha-bodies, the Primordial Wisdoms, and the resultant activities of the Buddha mind:

1) Ultimate Body—The cessation of elaborations and the supreme source of manifestation.

  A) *The Primordial Wisdom of the Ultimate Sphere*—The dissolution of the universal ground into the ultimate sphere. The knowledge of the essence of the ultimate nature, and the cessation of elaborations.

2) Enjoyment Body—Appears as the five classes of Buddhas

  A) *The Mirror-like Primordial Wisdom*—The dissolution of the consciousness of the universal ground into the ultimate sphere. The knowledge of the nature of phenomena as luminous absorption.

3) Manifested Body—For impure beings it appears in three forms as:

  The Manifested Body of Art—in the form of enlightened scriptures, art, music, etc., as the objects of generation towards enlightenment.

  The Manifested Body of Birth—in the form of the birth of noble and compassionate beings to protect and guide aspirants towards enlightenment.

  The Manifestation as the Supreme Enlightened One—the manifestation of sages who carry out the twelve enlightened acts.

  A) *The Primordial Wisdom of Discriminative and Accomplishment Wisdom*—The dissolution of the defiled mind into the ultimate sphere. The knowledge of all of the details of phenomena without confusion is the Discriminative Primordial Wisdom. The knowledge of all knowable phenomena is the Primordial Wisdom of Accomplishment.

4) Great Blissful Body—The omnipresent essence of the Bodies of Manifestation.

A) *The Primordial Wisdom of Equanimity*—The dissolution of mind-consciousness into the ultimate sphere. The knowledge of everything as equalness and one flavor.

5)   Vajra-body—the manifestation of the Body of Enlightenment; nondual, immutable, and totally liberated
    A) All of the foregoing Wisdoms are present:

The Primordial Wisdom of the Ultimate Sphere; The Mirror-like Primordial Wisdom; The Primordial Wisdom of Discriminative and Accomplishment Wisdom; and The Primordial Wisdom of Equanimity.[238]

The Buddha activities are the manifestative play of the Primordial Wisdom of Accomplishment. These activities spontaneously appear everywhere for those who are trainable in the practice of enlightenment.

Dzogpa Chenpo – Primordial Wisdoms

The clarity and beauty of Longchen Rabjam's vision represents nothing less than the elevation and metamorphosis of egoic-being into fully spiritualized and functioning Buddhahood. Achieving the Ultimate Body, realizing and actualizing the Buddha Wisdoms and Activities, is the basis for spiritualized being in the world. Consciousness arising in ultimate simplicity, in necessary union with dualistic defilement, provides the seed, the path, and fruition for Buddhahood. Longchen Rabjam's transcendental view of our divine purpose as enlightened beings is, when realized, numinous, compassionate and glorious.

There are three specific primordial wisdoms of the Buddha-Bodies: The Primordial Wisdom-at-the-basis of the Ultimate Body, endowed with characteristics of the Enjoyment Body, and of omnipresence of the Manifested Body:

The Ultimate Body
    Essence: The essence of the Ultimate Body being free from conceptions and expressions is the great purity from its origin.

Characteristic: The inconceivable is the
                                  characteristic of the Ultimate Body.

Presence: The Ultimate Body appears free
                                  from characteristics like space.

Buddha-field: The Buddha-field of the Ultimate
                                  Body is pure in origin and free of
                                  concepts.

Disciple: The disciple of the Ultimate Body
                                  is the Intrinsic Awareness which
                                  transcends movement and effort.

The Enjoyment Body
      Essence: The essence of the Enjoyment Body
                                  because of its being free from
                                  extremes or concepts is the great
                                  spontaneity.

Characteristic: The clarity without concepts is the
                                  characteristic of the Enjoyment
                                  Body.

Presence: The Enjoyment Body appears free
                                  from mortal form, like a rainbow.

Buddha-field: The Buddha-field of the Enjoyment
                                  Body is the clarity of the five
                                  Buddha-Bodies and Primordial
                                  Wisdoms.

Disciple: The disciples of the Enjoyment
                                  Body are the self-appearances of
                                  the assemblies of masters and
                                  disciples.

The Manifested Body

Essence:	The essence of the Manifested Body because it is compassion is the basis of the arising of appropriate manifestations.
Characteristic:	The manifestation in various forms is the characteristic of the Manifested Body.
Presence:	The Manifested Body is present in indefinite and various forms.
Buddha-field:	The Buddha-field of the Manifested Body is the multitude of beings acquiring knowledge of enlightenment
Disciple:	The disciples of the Manifested Body are the ordinary beings of the six realms.

Perfection of Confidence:

1) By perfecting the virtues of abandoning and realization the three Buddha-Bodies are attained.

2) The perfection of the three Buddha-Bodies for the fulfillment of the wishes of others is like a wish-fulfilling gem.

3) The perfection of the Ultimate Body is the freedom of the immutable essence from conceptualization.

4) The perfection of the Enjoyment Body is self-clarity and the completion of the major and minor marks of the Buddha-Body.

5) The Perfection of the Manifested Body is the perfection of the dual purposes.

Activity: The activity of the disciple who has realized the Ultimate Body is the manifestation in the form of the Buddha-body for the benefit of others.[239]

Adi Da – Sahaj Samadhi

Adi Da describes with perfect clarity the awakening of consciousness to sahaj samadhi, *The Seventh Stage of Practice:*

> *Sahaj Samadhi Is the Conscious Awakening Of The Always Already State, Not At All Dependent On The conditional Activities Of Ascent (As In Fifth Stage conditional Nirvikalpa), and Not At All Dependent Upon (or Even Associated With) The Motive and The Tacit Effort Of Exclusion (As In Sixth Stage conditional Nirvikalpa Samadhi, Which Is Jnana Samadhi).*
>
> *Sahaj Samadhi Is Inherently Perfect Transcendental (and Inherently Spiritual) Divine Self-Realization (Not At All conditioned by Either the body-mind Or the ego-Based Ability To Exclude phenomenal states), and It Is Associated With The Native Certainty That What Is Realized Is That Which Is Always Already The Case (or The Unobstructed Divine, or Perfectly Subjective Being).* [240]

When all seeking and clinging cease, and luminous awareness is stabilized, sahaj samadhi is revealed as don Juan's *third point* and his *somersault of awareness into the miraculous,* or the Ultimate Body of Dzogpa Chenpo, and the Great Seal of the Mahamudra. Divine Ignorance or freedom from conceptualization, reveals the unobstructed Divine Being. We never truly know what each new moment brings, nor how we have arrived at our present apparent destination. Faith born of Divine Ignorance allows spontaneous Love-Bliss as our path with heart. Never having been anywhere, with nowhere to go, we live beyond the veil of knowledge with self-empowerment, compassion and wisdom. Adi Da elaborates the first of four stages of sahaj samadhi:

Sahaj Samadhi—First Stage

> *When (In the Way Of the Heart) Sahaj Samadhi (or Self-abiding Divine Recognition, and Its "Bright" Power Of Conversion and Dissolution) Is Demonstrated Primarily In The Descending Context Of The Circle, Sahaj Samadhi Is In The Divine Trans-figuration Stage.* [241]

Adi Da establishes the occurrence of the Transfiguration Stage of Sahaj Samadhi when the descending and physically oriented dimension of the body-mind is absorbed in the prior standing, immutable nondual essence of being.

Sahaj Samadhi—Second Stage

Adi Da elaborates the second of four stages of sahaj samadhi:

> *When (In the Way Of the Heart) Sahaj Samadhi (or Self-abiding Divine Recognition, and Its "Bright" Power Of Conversion and Dissolution) Is Demonstrated Via A Process More Generalized In Both the Descending and the Ascending Dimensions Of The Circle, Sahaj Samadhi Is In The Divine Transformation Stage.*[242]

Adi Da establishes the occurrence of the Transformation Stage of Sahaj Samadhi when the ascending and descending dimension of the body-mind is absorbed in the prior standing, immutable nondual essence of being.

Sahaj Samadhi—Third Stage

Adi Da elaborates the third of four stages of sahaj samadhi:

> *When (In the Way Of the Heart) Sahaj Samadhi (or Self-abiding Divine Recognition, and Its "Bright" Power Of Conversion and Dissolution) Is Demonstrated Primarily In Amrita Nadi* [243] *Itself, and Even Often In The Heart's Free "Self-Gaze", and, Therefore, Only Minimally In the Circle (or The Arrow),*[244] *and Even Such that The Spirit-Current In The Circle (and the Arrow) Tends To Become Strongly Drawn Up (either Via The Spinal Line Or Via The Arrow) Toward The Crown Of the head (or, Otherwise, such That The Spirit-Current Is, Simply, Not "Expressed" Toward, or Radiated Into, The Circle, or The Arrow, Of the body-mind), Then Sahaj Samadhi Is In the Divine Indifference Stage.*[245]

Adi Da establishes the occurrence of the Divine Indifference Stage of Sahaj Samadhi when consciousness is established in the prior standing, immutable nondual essence of being, with only minimal perception of the ascending and descending perceptions of awareness. The Spirit-Current, the free and unobstructed self-radiant bliss-feeling and bliss-presence of being, stands indifferent to the ascending and descending currents of the circle of the body-mind (or the cosmic mandala).

Sahaj Samadhi—Fourth Stage

Adi Da elaborates the perfection of sahaj samadhi:

And Whenever (In The Way Of the Heart) Sahaj Samadhi (or Self-Abiding Divine Recognition, and Its "Bright" Power Of Conversion and Dissolution) Is Demonstrated Merely (and Inherently Most Perfectly) At (and As) the Heart Itself (Inherently, and Inherently Most Perfectly, Prior To attention, or All "Difference", and Standing, Divinely "Bright", Without Exclusion, Even, Apparently, In and As Amrita Nadi, and Even, It May Appear, With The Spirit-Current Shining Full At, and Even Infinitely Above, The Crown Of the head, Rather Than "anywhere" Descended In The Circle, The Arrow, or The Cosmic Domain), Then Sahaj Samadhi Is (At Least Temporarily) Moksha-Bhava Samadhi (or Brahma-Bhava). And Moksha-Bhava Samadhi (or The Divinely Perfect Demonstration Of The Perfectly Subjective and Perfectly Non-Exclusive "Brightness" Of The Heart) Is, Ultimately (and Inherently Most Perfectly, and Finally, or Permanently), Demonstrated As The Divinely Perfect Outshining Of all and All (In The Divine Translation Stage Of The Demonstration Of The Way Of The Heart In The Seventh Stage Of Life).[246]

In the Mahamudra tradition, "the meditator has achieved the rainbow-like physical transformation of his mortal body into the illusory form of awareness [jnana-rupakaya]," and, "his mind has transformed itself into lucid awareness [dharmakaya], and "perceives the countless Buddha realms." [247] Adi Da delineates the "Bright", as the essence of Love-Bliss prior to all, in which the cosmic domain and the divine Person are apparently arising. Divine Translation is the perfection of God Realization:

—Divine Translation Is the Sign Of the Divinely Perfect Conversion and Dissolution Of All Apparent (or conditionally Manifested) energies (and All conditional, or conditionally Manifested, Appearances) Via Divine Recognition, To The Degree That The Inherent (and Perfectly Subjective) Radiance Of Transcendental (and Inherently Spiritual, or "Bright") Divine Being Outshines Its Own Objective Appearances (and, Thus, Translates Its Own Illusions Into Its Own Self, or Perfectly Subjective Domain).[248]

The Translation of the conditional illusions into the Perfectly Subjective Domain, is the equivalent of the Mahamudra meditator perceiving the countless Buddha realms. The fully awakened meditator directly perceives the luminous ground of being and realizes Divine Being. For The God Realized Divine Person, Adi Da reveals and affirms the nature of birth, life, and death, and The Great Purpose of Self-Transcendence:

Death Is Simply the Relinquishment Of Association With the present Cosmic plane, and the personal form in that plane, Just As birth Is The Initiation Of Association With plane and form. Birth Occurs When Particular conditional Tendencies Create The Opportunity For Association With particular conditions. Death Occurs, By The Intervention Of Structural Laws Of Cosmic Nature, When present conditions Are No Longer Sufficient For Basic Support Of the conditional life-functions.

Even So, birth and death Are Primarily and Necessarily Associated With The Great Purpose Of self-Transcendence (and Growth Beyond conditional limits). Therefore, The Primary (or Great) Purpose Of birth, life, and death (If they arise) Is Transcendental (and Inherently Spiritual) Divine Self-Awakening (or Realization Of The "Bright"), Which Progressively Demonstrates Itself As Divine Transfiguration, Divine Transformation, Divine Indifference, and Ultimately (or Finally), Divine Translation (or The Outshining Of The Apparent Objective or Cosmic Domain By and In The Perfectly Subjective and Most Perfectly Divine Self-domain).[249]

The Dawn Horse Testament, Adi Da's quintessential song of God realization, delivers the ultimate truth of being:

The Seventh Stage Practice Is (Simply, Effortlessly, and Inherently, or Always Already) To Be The Native Condition Of Self-Radiant Consciousness (In, Of, and As Whom, and Not Merely To Whom, all objects, all states, and Even The Sense or Feeling Of Relatedness Itself Are arising, As Transparent, or Merely Apparent, Unnecessary, and Non-Binding Modifications Of Itself).[250]

In this passage Adi Da clearly indicates the equivalent of the Mahamudra's yoga of nonmeditation. This is a nondual realization of the abiding nature of the mind as being empty of an evolved essence, detached from subjective designations of subject and object, and is unaffected by apparent modifications of itself.

Adi Da raises the seventh stage realization beyond the cosmic mandala. The meditator having realized the abiding nature of mind, and having achieved the rainbow like physical transformation of his mortal body into the illusory form of awareness [jnana-rupakaya] and having had his mind transform itself into lucid awareness [dharmakaya], is in union with divine being:

"Just So, The Final Stage Of Recognition Of The Divine Person (As The Star In The Center Of The Cosmic Mandala) Is Not Full (or Fulfilled) Until Translation (Through and Beyond The Objective Divine Star,

Outshining The Cosmic Domain, Releasing All Conditional forms or Modifications To The Degree Of Unobstructed Radiance and Establishment In The Subjective Divine Domain)." [251]

With stunning poetic beauty Adi Da reveals the identity of the meditator, The Divine Person, the position in consciousness, The Star In The Center of The Cosmic Mandala, and the now fully awakened luminous awareness in Unobstructed Radiance and Establishment In The God-Realized Divine Domain. While many seventh stage songs of realization point towards enlightenment, the depth of Adi Da's vision is without parallel. For the meditator who has assimilated the four samadhis of Adi Da there is extraordinary clarity and depth of meaning for enlightenment and the mastery of awareness. The meditator having cut the root of egoic-self-construction stands free in the center of spiritualized, love-bliss being. Having fully identified with the divine spirit of being, the meditator can now fully assume the ultimate path.

Adi Da – Moksha-Bhava Samadhi

Adi Da, continuing in one of the most mystical revelations humanity has ever heard, sings of the fully awake, and divinely revealed depth of Moksha-Bhava Samadhi. Having united the luminous awareness of meditation with the *Divine Love-Bliss* that appeared spontaneously, the realizer is permanently established in the *Divine Domain*. *Divine Translation* may or may not be realized in one lifetime, even after having become established in Sahaj Samadhi. Fully established Divine Translation, Moksha-Bhava Samadhi, will occur, if not in the present lifetime—after one or more future lifetimes.

Adi Da reveals *The Divine Star, Divine Love-Bliss, Divine Transfiguration,*[252] *Divine Transformation,* and *Divine Translation* as the only perfect vehicle for perfect God union:

Ultimately (and In Any Case), the Visible or Apparently Objective Divine Star Is Simply The Ultimate Visible or Objective Sign Of The "Bright" Inherent Love-Bliss or Self-Radiance Of Transcendental (and Inherently Spiritual) Divine Being. Therefore, In The Context Of the Seventh Stage Of Life, the moment to moment "Practice" (or Demonstration-Process) Of the Way Of The Heart Is Not Especially A Matter Of Perceiving The Visible Divine Star (As An Apparently Objective Vision). Rather, It Is Fundamentally A Matter Of Relaxing *(or Relinquishing) the body-mind (and all of its conditional relations) Into the "Bright" (or The Divinely Self-Radiant Love-Bliss Which Is The Heart-Identity or Native State Of Even The Apparently Objective Divine Star). This <u>Spontaneously</u> (and Not Strategically) Produces The Signs Of Divine Transfiguration, Divine Transformation, and Divine Indifference, Culminating In Divine Translation (Which Is The Perfectly Subjective Self-Outshining Of all Apparent conditional Modifications, The Utter Transcendence Of The Tendency to Contract, Rather Than To shine, and The Final Assertion and Demonstration Of Freedom From The Tendency To Allow The Freely Self-Existing and Self-Radiant Being To Be Limited conditionally).*[253]

EPILOGUE

The seed, the path, and the fruition of God-Realization are enfolded within the intrinsic nature of consciousness. The nonmeditation yoga of the Mahamudra, and especially Adi Da's Moksha-Bhava-Samadhi, are revelations of the Spirit of Divine Being. When attention is trapped by the doings or projections of mind (civilization, culture, religion, money, sex, and power, etc.), we become entranced with the material world. In truth, the material world is not separate from consciousness, but rather the illusory and non-binding manifestation of consciousness. Final satisfaction is never secured through material possession. There is never ultimate security for the body-mind, because the body-mind does not exist absolutely. The body-mind is an apparently related, time-space projection in consciousness. The ultimate ground of our luminous being is the ancient, and paradoxically timeless, Divine One.

The primary dualism, apparent separation into subject and object is the root of self-based anxiety. We truly can never know what is happening in any apparent moment of time, because experience can never become an objectified reality. The world arises in consciousness through a mysterious tension or vibration of the Divine Consciousness or Love-Bliss Feeling Of Being. Without this vibrational aspect of Consciousness our world would not become manifest. We would not only be without dimension, but absolutely nonexistent, as well. The Illusory-Body Of Being, The Rainbow Body, and The Divine Person are transcendental revelations in consciousness revealed at the juncture of meditative absorption and discerning awareness. The obscuration in consciousness prior to enlightenment is the means of establishing Divine Play. If we were to exist in the form of the popular notion of God, not only would we be all knowing and all powerful, we would be all fulfilled, existing beyond time and space, without apparent dimension and God-Self-Reference. Without the illusion of time and dimension the luminous light of consciousness could not become manifest as the egoic-self, and ultimately, through meditation and Grace, Divinely Aware.

When the Light Of God in Consciousness is Revealed, then By Grace, Divine Faith coemerges with Divine Being, and The Divine

Person radiates in Divine Wisdom and Divine Love. Each and Every apparent moment of Love-Bliss-Feeling is in Union with Divine Ignorance and Divine Faith.

We, The Ancient One, exist as the infinite Buddha-Fields. Every apparent manifestation of The Eternal One is intrinsically in union with The Nondual Feeling Of Being. Our apparent separation from the Divine Ground Of Being becomes manifest as the apparently dual cosmic realm when sacrificial separation from God or Oneness is initiated in the birth of the egoic-self. Return or dissolution of the wave of being into the ocean of God does not mean death, as is commonly believed, but rather revitalization prior to rebirth as the time-space self-projection and play in consciousness of The Divine One.

The Divine Person, paradoxically arising within and as the Cosmic Mandala, is eternally in union with The Transcendentally Divine Love-Bliss Feeling Of Being. Our awakening as the eternally Divine Spiritual Self heralds the emergence of infinite Love and discerning wisdom. Upon awakening to at-Onement as The Divine Person we no longer become separated into fear and anxiety through projections of the egoic self. The transformation death of the egoic self and re-emergence of The Divine Person is our first step in compassionate and luminous empowerment. The dawning of the infinite vastness of Love-Bliss heralds the return of the Divine Person, Buddha or God-Realized Being—He/She once again—having come to Serve.

BIBLIOGRAPHY

Benoit, Hubert. The Supreme Doctrine: Psychological encounters in Zen thought. (New York: Inner Traditions International, 1984)

Castaneda, Carlos. The Teachings Of Don Juan A Yaqui Way Of Knowledge (New York: Simon & Schuster, 1968)
_____. A Separate Reality. (New York: Simon & Schuster, 1971)
_____.Journey To Ixtlan. (New York: Simon & Schuster, 1972)
_____.Tales of Power. (New York: Washington Square Press, 1974)
_____. The Second Ring of Power. (New York: Simon & Schuster, 1977)
_____.The Eagle's Gift. (New York: Simon & Schuster, 1981)
_____.The Fire From Within. (New York: Simon & Schuster, 1984)
_____.The Power Of Silence. (New York: Simon & Schuster, 1987)

Cleary, Thomas. Entry Into The Inconceivable: An Introduction To Hua-Yen Buddhism (Honolulu: University of Hawaii)
_____. trans. The Flower Ornament Scripture, Volume II (Boston: Shambhala Publications)

Dyczkowski, Mark S.G. The Doctrine of Vibration. (Albany: State University of New York, 1987)

Galland, China. Longing for Darkness: Tara and the Black Madonna (Viking Penguin)

Goddard, Dwight., translator. Self Realization Of Noble Wisdom: The Lankavatara Sutra (Clearlake: CA, The Dawn Horse Press)

Jee, Swami Lakshman. Kashmir Shaivism: The Secret Supreme (Albany: State University of NY Press, Under the imprint of The Universal Shaiva Trust)

John, Da Free. (now know as Adi Da Samraj, a.k.a., Da Avabhasa, Bubba Free John) Easy Death. (Clearlake, CA: The Dawn Horse Press, 1983)

_____. The Dawn Horse Testament. (Clearlake, CA: The Dawn Horse Press, 1985)

_____. The Dawn Horse Testament, New Standard Edition (Clearlake, CA: The Dawn Horse Press, 1991)

_____. Love-Ananda Gita (The Free Song of Love-Bliss) The "Perfect Summary" of "Radical" Advaitayana Buddhism. (San Rafael, CA: The Dawn Horse Press, 1986)

Jung, Carl. Man and His Symbols, "Approaching the Unconscious" (Garden City, N.Y.: Doubleday)

Kalupahana, David J. Nagarjuna: The Philosophy of the Middle Way (Albany: State University of New York)

Lhalungpa, Lobsang P. Tibetan translator. Mahamudra: The Quintessence Of Mind And Meditation, author Takpo Tashi Namgyal. (Boston: Shambala Publications)

Meyer, Marvin, trans. The Secret Teachings Of Jesus: Four Gnostic Gospels. (NY: Vintage Books)

Miller, Barbara Stoler. The Bhagavad-Gita: Krishna's Counsel in Time of War (Bantam Classic)

Muller-Ortega, Paul Eduardo. The Triadic Heart of Siva (Albany: State University of New York)

Nagao, Gadjin. The Foundational Standpoint of Madhyamika Philosophy (Albany: State University of New York Press)

Osborne, A. Editor. The Collected Works of Ramana Maharshi (London: Rider)

Rinpoche, Tulku Thondup. Buddha Mind: An Anthology of Longchen Rabjam's Writings on Dzogpa Chenpo (Ithaca, NY: Snow Lion Publications)

Rajneesh, Bhagwan Shree. Meditation: The Art of Ecstasy, Edited by Ma Satya Bharti (New York, Hagerstown, San Francisco, London 11: Perennial Library, Harper & Row Publishers, 1978)

Silburn, Lilian. Kundalini: Energy of the Depths (Albany: State University of New York Press, 1988)

Wilber, Ken. The Spectrum of Consciousness. (Wheaton, Ill: Theosophical Publishing House, 1977)

Williams, Donald Lee. Border Crossings, A Psychological Perspective on Carlos Castaneda's Path of Knowledge, (Toronto, Canada, Inner City Books, 1981)

INDEX TO THE FOUR YOGAS

NOTES

[1] Castaneda, Carlos; *Tales Of Power* (New York, NY: Washington Square Press, 1974) p. 77

[2] Castaneda, Carlos, *The Fire From Within* (New York, N.Y.: Simon & Schuster, Inc., 1984), p 126

[3] *Self-Realization Of Noble Wisdom: The Lankavatara Sutra*, compiled by Dwight Goddard on the basis of D.T. Suzuki's rendering from the Sanskrit and Chinese (Clearlake, CA: The Dawn Horse Press, 1983), p. 17

[4] Castaneda, Carlos, *The Active Side of Infinity* (New York, NY: HarperCollins Publishers, 1998), pp. 104-105

[5] Castaneda, Carlos, *The Fire From Within* (New York, N.Y.: .Simon & Schuster, Inc., 1984), p 178

[6] Namgyal, Takpo Tashi, translator: Lhalungpa, Lobsang P., *Mahamudra: The Quintessence of Mind And Meditation* (Boston & London: Shambala, 1986), p. 63

[7] Castaneda, Carlos; *Tales Of Power* (New York, NY: Washington Square Press, 1974) p. 208

[8] Da Avabhasa, *The Dawn Horse Testament,* New Standard Edition (Clearlake, CA: The Dawn Horse Press 1991), p.522

[9] Ibid, p. 588

[10] Castaneda, Carlos; *Tales Of Power*, p. 231

[11] Da Free John, *Easy Death* (Clearlake, CA: The Dawn Horse Press, 1983), p. 50

[12] Adi Da, *Love-Ananda Gita (The Free Song of Love-Bliss) The "Perfect Summary" of "Radical" Advaitayana Buddhism.* 'Radical' as defined in this edition's Notes: "The 'Radical' or irreducible Process directly and immediately penetrates or transcends the ego at its fundamental root origin, the self-contraction at the heart." (San Rafael, CA: The Dawn

Horse Press) 1986, p. 271

[13] *The Dawn Horse Testament* 1991, p. 48. Adi Da clarifies the capitalization of certain words in his *Testament of Secrets*.
"This Testament is My Intention to Awaken the Consciousness of every being to its Ultimate Real (and necessarily Divine) Condition.
  The uppercase words express the Ecstatic "Vision" of Heart-Significance. And the lowercase words (which appear only occasionally, like the uppercase words in common speech and writing) achieve, by their infrequency, a special significance as indicators of conditional or limited existence."

[14] *The Dawn Horse Testament,* 1991, p. 585

[15] *The Dawn Horse Testament,* 1991, p. 586

[16] *The Doctrine Of Vibration,* pp. 71

[17] *The Doctrine Of Vibration,* pp. 71-72

[18] *The Dawn Horse Testament,* 1991 p. 608

[19] Goddard, Dwight. *Self-Realization of Noble Wisdom: The Lankavatara Sutra* (Clearlake, CA: The Dawn Horse Press), p. 17

[20] *Mahamudra: The Quintessence of Mind And Meditation,* p. 354

[21] *The Dawn Horse Testament,* 1991 p. 356

[22] *The Dawn Horse Testament,* 1991 p. 357

[23] Avabhasa ("The "Bright") Rose Incense
http://adidam.com/emporium/sacred/home.htm

[24] Eno, Brian. *Thursday Afternoon,* (South Plainfield, NJ: Jem Records, Inc. 1984) Compact disc, cassette, VHS. [Mail Order: Backroads Distributors, 417 Tamal Plaza, Corte Madera, CA 94925 1-800-825-4848]

[25] *Mahamudra,* p. 359

[26] Meyer, Marvin W., translated by. *The Secret Teachings Of Jesus: The Four Gnostic Gospels* (New York: Vintage Books, 1984) The Gospel Of Thomas, Saying 20, p. 23

[27] *Tales of Power,* p. 127

[28] Mahamudra, p. 232

[29] *Tales of Power,* p. 127

[30] Wilber, Ken, *The Spectrum Of Consciousness.* (Wheaton, Illinois: The Theosophical Publishing House, 1985), p. 116

[31] *The Dawn Horse Testament,* p. 609

[32] *Mahamudra,* p. 223

[33] Sanskrit; Devi—synonymous with dakini

[34] *The Triadic Heart of Siva,* Paul Eduardo Muller-Ortega. (The State University Of New York Press, 1989) p. 82

[35] *The Dawn Horse Testament,* 1985 p. 704

[36] *The Dawn Horse Testament,* 1991 pp. 702-3

[37] Lakshman, Swami Jee. *Kashmir Shaivism: The Secret Supreme* (Albany: State University of NY Press, Under the imprint of The Universal Shaiva Trust, 1988), pp. 1-9

[38] Dyczkowski, Mark S.G., *The Doctrine of Vibration: An Analysis of the Doctrine and Practices of Kashmir Shaivism* (Albany: State University of NY Press, 1987), p. 151

[39] ibid p. 158

[40] Dyczkowski, Mark S.G. *The Doctrine of Vibration: An Analysis of the Doctrine and Practices of Kashmir Shaivism* (State University of NY Press, 1987), p. 180

[41] ibid. Tantraloka, 1/246-7

[42] ibid, p. 47

[43] *The Triadic Heart of Siva,* Paul Eduardo Muller-Ortega (The State University Of New York Press, 1989), p. 86

[44] Cleary, Thomas. *Entry Into The Inconceivable: An Introduction To Hua-Yen Buddhism* (Honolulu: University Of Hawaii Press, 1983) pp. 23-24

[45] Silburn, Lilian. *Kundalini: Energy of the Depths* (Albany: State University of New York Press, 1988) p. 5

[46] *The Doctrine of Vibration*, p. 166

[47] *The Doctrine of Vibration*, p. 214

[48] *Longing For Darkness: Tara And The Black Madonna*, pp. 163-166

[49] Silburn, Lilian. *Kundalini: The Energy Of The Depth.* (Albany: State University of New York Press, 1988), pp. 44-47

[50] nadi; channels not corresponding to any physiological reality. The imagined channel on the right (pingala) side of the body corresponds to hatred, the left (ida) to attachment. Mindfulness of breathing leads to cessation of the movement in the corresponding channels of mind (citti). When awareness enters the center channel (susumna), cosmic consciousness is experienced.

[51] kundalini—energy of breath (bringing about the centering of the universe within); nadi—a subtle conduit.

[52] pranava; the primeval word, OM

[53] *The Doctrine of Vibration*, p. 97

[54] ibid p.97 (footnote ref. To Isvara-pratyabhijna-vimarsini p. 108)

[55] ibid p. 97 (footnote ref. To Isvara-pratyabhijnana-vivrtimarsini p. 286)

[56] Castaneda, Carlos, *The Fire From Within*, p. 143

[57] *The Fire From Within*, p. 295

[58] Kalupahana, David J, *Nagarjuna: The Philosophy Of The Middle Way* (State University of New York Press), pp. 339-340

[59] Nagao, Gadjin, *The Foundational Standpoint of Madhyamika Philosophy* (Albany: State University of New York Press 1989), p. 62

[60] *Mahamudra: The Quintessence of Mind And Meditation,* p. 393

[61] Castaneda, Carlos, *Journey To Ixtlan* (New York: Simon and Schuster. 1972), p. 191

[62] Carlos Castaneda, *Journey To Ixtlan* (New York: Simon and Schuster. 1972), p. 189

[63] Carlos Castaneda. *The Power of Silence: Further Lessons of don Juan* (New York: Simon & Schuster, 1987), p. 185

[64] *Mahamudra: The Quintessence of Mind And Meditation,* p. 60

[65] *Mahamudra: The Quintessence of Mind And Meditation,* p. 53

[66] *Mahamudra,* p. 53

[67] ibid p. 322

[68] *Journey To Ixtlan,* p. 138

[69] *Journey To Ixtlan,* p. 191

[70] Ibid p. 259

[71] Miller, Barbara Stoller, translator, *The Bhagavad-Gita,* (New York: Bantam Books, 1986), P. 31, II, 16

[72] *Mahamudra.* p. 183

[73] The socialized person.

[74] All that is unconscious in man and only indirectly perceived.

[75] Donald Lee Williams. *Border Crossings, A Psychological Perspective on Carlos Castaneda's Path of Knowledge* (Toronto, Canada: Inner City Books, 1981), p. 101

[76] *Mahamudra,* p. 193

[77] *Mahamudra,* p. 244

[78] Ibid p. 245

[79] Ibid p. 260

[80] Tulku Thondup Rinpoche. *Buddha Mind: An Anthology of Longchen Rabjam's Writing on Dzogpa Chenpo* (Ithaca, New York; Snow Lion Publications), p. 97

[81] Castaneda, Carlos, *A Separate Reality: Further Conversations With Don Juan* (NY: Simon & Schuster, 1971), pp. 1-2

[82] Carlos Castaneda. *Tales Of Power* (New York: Pocket Books/Washington Square Press, 1974), p. 231

[83] *The Power of Silence*, p. 249

[84] *Mahamudra*, p. xxxii

[85] *The Dawn Horse Testament*, 1991, p. 605

[86] Carlos Castaneda. *Journey To Ixtlan*, (New York: Simon and Schuster. 1972), P. 92

[87] Donald Lee Williams. *Border Crossings, A Psychological Perspective on Carlos Castaneda's Path of Knowledge* (Toronto, Canada, Inner City Books, 1981), p. 102

[88] Carlos Castaneda. *The Power of Silence*, p. 215

[89] Da Free John. *Easy Death*, p. 74

[90] Da Free John. *Easy Death*, pp. 286-7

[91] mandala; circle. Often an artistic representation of concentric levels of psycho-physical reality.

[92] Castaneda, Carlos. *The Eagle's Gift*, p. 296

[93] Donald Lee Williams. *Border Crossings*, p. 111

[94] Carlos Castaneda, *Journey To Ixtlan*, p. 225

[95] Carlos Castaneda, *The Second Ring of Power,* p. 157

[96] Carlos Castaneda, *The Second Ring of Power,* p. 194

[97] Carl Jung. 'Approaching the Unconscious', in *Man and His Symbols*

[98] *The Black Madonna,* p. 144

[99] Williams, Donald Lee. *Border Crossings,* p. 35. (Creation Myths, Marie-Louise von Franz, p.135)

[100] *Mahamudra,* p. 252

[101] *Transpersonal Psychologies,* Edited by Charles Tart. (El Cerrito, CA. Psychological Processes, Inc. 1983) p. 235

[102] Undeniably it is a major difficulty for someone experiencing mental disability to select an appropriate school of therapy, and especially a self-actualized therapist. Common sense guidelines for the selection of a therapist are not much different than those for any other major life decision. Gather as much information as you can from as many references as you can find, utilizing personal and professional referrals, libraries, the local university psychology department, etc. Interview your candidates, looking for warmth, wisdom, compassion, and especially look for someone you intuitively like and trust. Bring along a trusted companion. Determine beforehand the type of treatment indicated, duration and the estimated cost. Next—seek another evaluation. Continue your search until you find a path with heart.

[103] *The Dawn Horse Testament,* 1991, p. 618

[104] Bhagwan Shree Rajneesh. *Meditation: The Art of Ecstasy,* Edited by Ma Satya Bharti (New York, Hagerstown, San Francisco, London: Perennial Library, Harper & Row Publishers, 1978), pp. 214-215

[105] *Mahamudra: The Quintessence of Mind And Meditation,* p. 50

[73] *Mahamudra: The Quintessence of Mind And Meditation,* p. 165

[107] *The Dawn Horse Testament of Heart-Master Da Free John* (San Rafel, CA: The Dawn Horse Press, 1985), p. 432

[108] *Tales of Power*, p. 13

[109] Hubert Benoit. *The Supreme Doctrine* (New York: Viking Press, 1955), pp. 33-4

[110] Wilber, Ken. *The Spectrum Of Consciousness* (Wheaton, Illinois. Theosophical Publishing house, 1977) pp. 122-123

[111] Carlos Castaneda. *The Second Ring of Power*, p. 296

[112] Carlos Castaneda. *The Second Ring of Power*, p. 156

[113] Carlos Castaneda. *The Fire From Within*, p. 126

[114] David J. Kalupahana. *Nagarjuna: The Philosophy of the Middle Way* (Albany: State University of New York Press, 1986), p. 230

[115] *Mahamudra*, p. 183

[116] *The Flower Ornament Scripture*, Vol. I, p. 294

[117] *Mahamudra*, p. 192

[118] *The Mahamudra*, p. 214

[119] *The Mahamudra*, p. 93

[120] *The Fire From Within*, pp. 289-290

[121] *The Second Ring of Power*, p. 265

[122] *The Second Ring of Power*, p. 273

[123] *The Second Ring of Power*, p. 309

[124] David J. Kalupahana. *Nagarjuna: The Philosophy of the Middle Way*, p. 234

[125] *Mahamudra: The Quintessence of Mind And Meditation*, p. 356

[126] *Mahamudra: The Quintessence of Mind And Meditation*, p. 386

[127] *Mahamudra: The Quintessence of Mind And Meditation,* p. 60

[128] *The Dawn Horse Testament,* 1991. p. 522

[129] *Mahamudra,* p. lix

[130] *Mahamudra: The Quintessence of Mind And Meditation,* p. 223

[131] ibid p. 223

[132] *Mahamudra: The Quintessence of Mind And Meditation,* p. 224

[133] *The Dawn Horse Testament of Heart-Master Da Free John* (San Rafel, CA: The Dawn Horse Press, 1985), p. 268

[134] *The Dawn Horse Testament of Heart-Master Da Free John* (San Rafel, CA: The Dawn Horse Press, 1985), p. 553

[135] *Mahamudra: The Quintessence of Mind And Meditation,* p. 362

[136] *Mahamudra,* p. 187

[137] *Mahamudra,* p. 207

[138] *Mahamudra,* p. 214

[139] *Buddha Mind,* p. 52

[140] Lobsang p. Lhalungpa. *Mahamudra: The Quintessence of Mind and Meditation,* p. 214

[141] Ibid. p. 225

[142] *Mahamudra: The Quintessence of Mind And Meditation,* p. 245

[143] *The Flower Ornament Scripture,* Vol. I, p. 378

[144] *The Dawn Horse Testament,* 1st edition, 1986, p. 611

[145] *Mahamudra: The Quintessence of Mind And Meditation,* p. 183

[146] *Mahamudra,* p. 206

[147] *Mahamudra,* p. 354

[148] Goddard, Dwight. *Self Realization Of Noble Wisdom: The Lankavatara Sutra* (Clearlake: CA, The Dawn Horse Press, 1983) p. 84

[149] *Mahamudra* p. 271 (Caturaksa Mahamudra)

[150] *The Power Of Silence,* p. 240

[151] Ibid, p.240

[152] *The Lankavatara Sutra,* p. 116

[153] *Mahamudra,* p. 352

[154] *The Dawn Horse Testament,* p. 596

[155] Adi Da. *The Dawn Horse Testament.* "The first stage of the perfect practice is identification with the Witness-Position of Consciousness. The second stage of the perfect practice is identification with consciousness itself. The third stage of the perfect practice is transcendence of all modifications in consciousness and identification with the Divine Self-Consciousness or Supreme Reality." p. 710

[156] *Mahamudra, p.* 331

[157] *The Free Daist,* Volume 2, Numbers 1 & 2, p. 56 'Perhaps the Wisdom-teaching should be withdrawn and maintained within an esoteric order, but not generally communicated or kept in print.'

[158] *Mahamudra,* p. 315

[159] *Mahamudra,* p. 307

[160] *Mahamudra,* p. 315

[161] *Mahamudra,* pp. 330-331

[162] *Mahamudra,* p. 331

[163] *Tales of Power,* p. 97

[164] *The Power of Silence,* p. 171

[165] *The Power Of Silence,* p. 174

[166] *The Power Of Silence,* p. 285

[167] Tulku Thondup Rinpoche. *Buddha Mind,* p. 296

[168] *Entry Into The Inconceivable,* p. 162

[169] Wilber, Ken; Engler, Jack; Brown, Daniel P. *Transformations Of Consciousness: Conventional and Contemplative Perspectives on Development.* (Boston & London: New Science Library Shambala, 1986) Daniel P. Brown, Ch. 8, The Stages of Meditation In Cross-Cultural Perspective, pp. 261-262

[170] Benoit, Hubert. *The Supreme Doctrine,* pp. 190-192

[171] Osborne, A. editor. *The Collected Works of Ramana Maharshi* (London: Rider, 1959), p. 20

[172] *Mahamudra,* p. 381

[173] *Buddha Mind,* p. 295

[174] *Tales of Power,* p. 212

[175] *Entry Into The Inconceivable,* p. 162

[176] Da Free John, *Easy Death,* p. 218

[177] ibid p. 318

[178] ibid p. 299

[179] ibid p. 188

[180] *Mahamudra,* p. 382

[181] *Mahamudra,* p. 382

[182] Ibid p. 365

[183] *A Separate Reality,* p. 85

[184] Castaneda, Carlos. *The Power Of Silence,* p. 244

[185] *The Divine Doctrine,* p. 209

[186] Netratantra 8/6-8a (quoted in *The Divine Doctrine*)

[187] Castaneda, Carlos. *The Power Of Silence,* p. 167

[188] *Entry Into The Inconceivable.* (quoted from *Scripture on the Light of Knowledge Adorning the Enlightened Entering the Sphere of Buddahood,* p. 547c (also from the Vimalakirtinirdesa scripture), p. 162

[189] *The Dawn Horse Testament,* Nov. 1991 p. 586

[190] *The Dawn Horse Testament,* p. 586

[191] John, Da Free. *The Love Ananda Gita: The Perfect Summary Of Radical Advaitayana Buddhism.* (Clearlake, CA: the Dawn Horse Press, 1986) p. 173 No. 323

[192] ibid p. 187

[193] *Mahamudra,* p. 357

[194] *Mahamudra,* p. 359

[195] *The Dawn Horse Testament,* p. 562

[196] *Mahamudra,* p. 384

[197] *Mahamudra,* p. 388

[198] Meyer, Marvin, trans. *The Secret Teachings Of Jesus: Four Gnostic Gospels.* (NY: Vintage books, 1984), pp. 23-24

[199] Tales Of Power, p. 128

[200] Tales Of Power, pp. 76-77

[201] Tales Of Power, pp. 77-78

[202] *Mahamudra*, p. 234

[203] *Mahamudra*, Takpo Tashi Namgyal p. 233

[204] Luminous awareness; Sanskrit. prabhasvarajnana

[205] Rinpoche, Tulku Thondup. *Buddha Mind: An Anthology of Longchen Rabjam's Writings on Dzogpa Chenpo* (Ithaca, NY: Snow Lion Publications, 1989) p. 136

[206] The supreme illusory form of the enlightened ones refers to the earthly (nirmanakaya) and mystical (sambhogakaya) manifestations. The highest mystical form (sambhogakaya) is a form of awareness which transcends the cosmic manifestation and realizes the human body as the supreme illusory form in consciousness. This supreme illusory form, or rainbow awareness, arises coemergently with the enlightened state of ultimate simplicity (dharmakaya).

[207] The Five Primordial Wisdoms are: (1) Mirror-like awareness, Sanskrit. adarsajnana (2) Even Awareness Skt. samatajnana (3) Discerning Awareness (4) Spontaneously fulfilling awareness Skt. krtyanusthanajnana (5) All encompassing expanse of awareness Skt. dharmadhatujnana

[208] The supreme emptiness of all forms; Skt. sarvakaravaropeta sunyata

[209] The path of noncultivation; Skt. asaiksamarga

[210] Supreme Illusory Form; Skt. visuddhimayakaya

[211] *Mahamudra*, p. 317

[212] *Entry Into The Inconceivable*, p. 162

[213] *Entry Into The Inconceivable*, p. 163 [Note: The net, a symbol of the sovereignty of the king, is said possibly to represent the ten stages of bodhisattvahood. The 'precious jewel' is the luminous mind, like a spherical mirror, the still mind, like a clear mirror, perceiving things as they are without the filter of conceptual thinking.]

[214] *Entry Into The Inconceivable*, p. 163 [Note: The seven treasures of a wheel-turning king (a universal monarch or sovereign lawgiver): a wife,

disk (a weapon or symbol of authority) jewels, army, treasury, elephants, horses. This is traditional lore and used only for metaphor.]

[215] *Buddha Mind*, p. 192

[216] The six objects of the senses: sound, smell, taste, touch, form, and mental events.

[217] John, Da Free. *The Da Upanishad*, (Clearlake, CA: The Dawn Horse Press, 1989), p. 309

[218] John, Da Free. *The Da Upanishad*. (Clearlake, CA: The Dawn Horse Press, 1989), pp. 312-313

[219] *The Dawn Horse Testament*, pp. 584-585

[220] *Mahamudra*, p. 323

[221] *Mahamudra*, p. 401

[222] *Mahamudra*, pp. 360-361

[223] ibid p. 395

[224] *Mahamudra*, p. 396

[225] *Mahamudra*, p. 460

[226] *The Power of Silence*, pp. 244-245

[227] *The Power of Silence*, p. 247

[228] Carlos Castaneda. *The Second Ring of Power* (New York: Simon & Schuster, 1977), p. 154

[229] Ibid p. 155

[230] Carlos Castaneda. *The Fire From Within*, p. 120

[231] *Mahamudra*, p. 368

[232] *The Dawn Horse Testament*, p. 657

[233] Cleary, Thomas. *Entry Into The Inconceivable: An Introduction To Hua-Yen Buddhism*, (Honolulu: University of Hawaii, 1983), p. 163

[234] Cleary, Thomas, trans. *The Flower Ornament Scripture*, (Boston: Shambala Publications, 1986),Volume II, pp. 334-335, p. 444

[235] *The Lankavatara Sutra*, p. 143

[236] *The Lankavatara Sutra*, pp. 164-165

[237] *The Lankavatara Sutra*, p. 166

[238] *Buddha Mind*, pp. 408-412

[239] *Buddha Mind*, pp. 414-420

[240] *The Dawn Horse Testament*, 1991 p. 599

[241] *The Dawn Horse Testament*, 1991 p. 630

[242] *The Dawn Horse Testament*, p. 630

[243] ibid. p. 728 Amrita Nadi: The root-structure of the body-mind, the current of immortal bliss.

[244] ibid. p. 729. The Arrow: 'a motionless axis that seems to stand in the center of the body, between the frontal and spinal lines.'

[245] *The Dawn Horse Testament*, p. 630

[246] The Dawn Horse Testament pp. 630-631

[247] *The Mahamudra*, p. 368

[248] *The Dawn Horse Testament*, pp. 633-634

[249] *The Dawn Horse Testament*, p. 647

[250] *The Dawn Horse Testament*, p. 625

[251] *The Dawn Horse Testament*, (1985) p. 636

[252] Adi Da, *The Love Ananda Gita*, (San Rafael, CA: The Dawn Horse Press, 1986) ff. p. 278, 'Transfiguration', generally the first phase of the Enlightened Yoga of the seventh stage of life, is the pervasion of the body-mind by the Radiance of the Divine Light. The process of Transfiguration expresses itself as Blessing in the context of all relations and experiences. 'Transformation', generally the second phase of the Enlightened Yoga of the seventh stage of life, spontaneously yields signs and psychic abilities such as the power to heal, longevity, mental genius, and the manifestation of true Wisdom and selfless Love.

[253] *The Dawn Horse Testament*, 1991, p. 657

Printed in the United States
28157LVS00007B/132